THE TUTTLE TWINS
—— and the case of the ——
BROKEN
WINDOW

CONNOR BOYACK

ILLUSTRATIONS BY ELIJAH STANFIELD

Libertas Press
2183 W Main Street, A102
Lehi, UT 84043

The Tuttle Twins and the Case of the Broken Window

Edited by Chris Jones

ISBN-13 978-1-943521-41-8 (paperback)

10 9 8 7 6 5 4 3 2

For bulk orders, send inquires to info@libertasutah.org.

Other titles by the author:

*Skip College: Launch Your Career Without
Debt, Distractions, or a Degree*

*Lessons from a Lemonade Stand: An Unconventional
Guide to Government*

*Feardom: How Politicians Exploit Your Emotions
and What You Can Do to Stop Them*

The Tuttle Twins children's book series

Emily gently pushed the door to Ethan's room as if she didn't really want to open it. But it wasn't latched, and it slid quietly inward over the carpet. Ethan sat on his bed, reading, his body coming slowly into view like a movie shot, a little at a time.

He looked up.

"That was Brayden on the phone," she said.

Ethan didn't react, but that was a reaction all by itself.

"He says one o'clock, if we want to show up."

"Do we want to show up?" Ethan said.

"I was trying to decide that myself. But then I thought it would be easier to decide if I was talking to you."

Ethan slid in a bookmark where his finger was and closed his book without a sound. He laid it on the bed and left his hand on it, almost like he was drawing strength from being in contact with it. *Charlie's Bat*, the title said. A baseball book. Coincidence.

"It's just baseball," Ethan said. "It's just a game."

"Baseball is not just a game," Emily said, leaning on the doorframe. "But even if it was, after this summer's debacle it wouldn't be any more."

"We have lost a lot of games," Ethan said, rubbing his chin.

"Yes," said Emily, "we have. Do you know how many?"

Ethan's face said he did not know, and didn't want to.

1

"Sixteen."

"Sixteen?" he said. "You're sure?"

"Oh, yes. I'm sure."

Ethan fixed his eyes on her. "You're thinking that losing seventeen in a row would make this summer the worst one in history, aren't you?"

Emily nodded. "But I'm also thinking that if we don't get the team together and go over there, we will have sixteen losses and no victories, which is almost as bad as seventeen losses."

"And we're not going to win if we don't play."

"Fair point."

Ethan levered himself up off the bed. He turned and smoothed out the blanket where he'd been sitting. "Then I should call the guys."

"See? I knew it would be easier to decide if I talked it over with you."

From the beginning, this game was different. For one, the weather wasn't perfect, but breezy and cloudy, with a threat of rain in the distance. That kept the sun out of the fielders' eyes, and Hannah did not drop the pop fly that would have had her backing away and covering her eyes during any other game.

The humidity was high and that seemed to take something off Brayden's curveball. Ethan whacked a run-scoring double into the corner rather than striking out, as he had last week. And the week before. Paul's ankle had healed and he beat out the grounder to short. Becca's new glove, the one she got for her birthday a few days ago, had padding on the palm, so that the scorching liner she would surely have dropped stuck in the webbing instead and kept Brayden's team from scoring.

One way or another, their team kept the score close instead of being blown out like usual. Out on the mound, Brayden was getting tired. He always pitched the whole game, but now he was struggling to get the last couple of outs. Clinging to a 6-4 lead, he'd gotten a fly ball from one player, but Ethan had crushed another curveball for a double, and Brayden had walked another player. The tying run was on base with only one out.

And Emily coming to bat.

She took her time about it. She scuffed her cleats in the brown soil next to home plate. Kneeling down, she took some of the dirt in her hands and rubbed them together, wiped her hands on her pants, and gave the bat a couple of practice swings before stepping in.

The clouds were serious now, off to the west over the river. Slashing rain cut the valley between the hills, between the cities of Spoonerville (where the Tuttles lived) and Malantown. Gusts carried loose grass over the field and tugged at Emily's cap. Ozone on the wind. Not much longer before the storm hit.

Long enough, though. Surely, long enough.

Emily stood in, bat cocked over her right shoulder. Jase played her shallow in right field, daring her to hit

it over his head. He knew she'd rather stroke it to left, where the vacant lot's ground was broken and uneven like a World War I battlefield, and a bad hop could roll down the hill and score those two precious runs. To the right, the tall, wood-slat fence was deep and the grass even, and only a perfect hit would find its way past Jase.

She twisted the bat in her hand. Ethan took his lead from second, dragging his left foot like an anchor.

"Come on, Em. This guy's all yours," Brock called from first, where he danced back and forth like a waving flag.

Brayden got the sign from the catcher and nodded. He stared at Emily.

She stared back. Licked her lips. He went into the windup.

Threw.

From the moment he released it, she knew it was outside. A ball. She should let it go.

But it was also coming in slow and belt-high, right where she liked it. Her hands began to move by themselves. In her dreams, she'd seen this pitch, and her body didn't care that her mind was telling it to hang on, that there'd be another one coming. This was the one.

She stepped forward, dropped her hands and locked her wrists, and let the head of the bat go.

The crack of the ball on the bat was the sweetest she could ever remember.

The ball rocketed out, straight at Jase, but climbing, climbing fast. His face had just time to register shock and dismay when the sphere ripped over his head toward the wall.

Still climbing.

Emily flipped the bat. Ethan threw his arms in the air, backpedaling toward third. Brock hadn't moved at first, just stood there, watching it. Brayden's head whipped around, his mouth in an O.

The ball cleared the fence with two feet to spare, and it was still rising.

"YEAAAAAAAAHHHH!" Ethan screamed, sixteen straight losses of redemption in his voice.

But Emily's home run trot stopped two paces out from the batter's box.

Over the right-field fence lay a small parking lot that was usually empty in the afternoons. It was the rectory parking for the Church of Our Lady of Lourdes, Spoonerville's oldest church, a tall, stone edifice half-covered in ivy. On the west face of the building, the stone surrounded a twenty-foot stained-glass window of the Virgin Mary. Everyone said the church had been built around that window. It was a hundred years old and probably the only tourist attraction in town.

At first, when they'd started playing there, a couple of the boys had been worried that a long fly might hit the church. But it was deep to right field and beyond the fence, the parking lot was thirty or more feet of blacktop, and the church was another ten feet beyond that. Besides, this was the only vacant lot big enough for a game. In five years of playing, no one had ever come close to hitting the Blessed Virgin.

Until now.

The ballfield emptied in seconds. No player had ever made a dash for home plate nearly as fast as they now dashed for their actual homes.

All except Emily, who stood right where she'd stopped running, staring in horror at the hole in the leg of a cherub.

And Ethan, who jogged over to stand next to his stricken sister.

"Nice hit," he said.

She punched him in the chest.

"Ow!" he said, rubbing it. "What'd I say? No one's ever hit a ball like that on this field."

"Look!" Emily said, her hand outstretched to the disaster. "I ruined the most expensive thing in this town! Who cares about the stupid baseball game!"

"It doesn't look too bad," Ethan said. "I'm sure someone can fix it. It's not a big hole."

But then, as they watched, another plate fell out. And another. A slow-motion catastrophe unfolded as the soft lead, unsupported by the pieces below, let go of its hold on the glass mosaic and dropped piece after priceless piece into the sacristy.

"Oh," Emily said, unable to make another sound.

It stopped, eventually, with a ragged hole now running from the bottom third of the huge window right to the top, a two-foot gash in the fifteen-foot tall scene.

"My life is over," Emily said.

"It's kind of unfortunate that it's not," Ethan said.

As yet, the afternoon remained quiet. No voices cried out, no sirens sounded, no trumpet of doom announced the end of the world. Softly, the patter of the rain crept down the valley and up the gentle rise to where two young people stood transfixed by the visible representation of their doom.

Eli, another player, quickly ran back to grab his bat before preparing to take off again. "You have to run," he said, a sense of urgency in his voice. "They'll find that any second, and when they do, they'll come looking for the perpetrator."

"I can't run," Emily said, dropping her face into her hands. "I can't move."

"Maybe we had better," Ethan said, tugging on her arm. "We can't stay here."

"How can I just leave?" she said. "I broke it. It's my fault."

"That's all great when you knocked over someone's mailbox or you tromped on one of their flowers," Eli said. "But this? Do you have any idea what that thing costs? You couldn't pay for it in a year. In ten years. You can't take the blame for this, or your life really is over."

Emily picked her head back up and stared at the rent in the picture. "But it's my fault. I can't just run away from that."

"You can and you will. Look, what did you do wrong? Nothing."

Emily wasn't listening, Eli could tell. He walked over in front of her where his head blocked the church. "Earth to Emily. Listen to me. What did you do? You hit a ball. You hit the holy whiffenpoof out of it. That's a good thing. You didn't mean to hit the church. Heck, Emily, no one even believed anyone could hit the church from here. If they thought there was a risk, they shouldn't have let us play here. They knew we used this field. If anyone's to blame, it's them."

Emily still wasn't focusing, but at least she couldn't see the disaster any more. Her eyes drifted downward and stayed there. "I didn't mean to," she said.

"Of course you didn't. And that's why you have to run. If you think about it, it's justice. You didn't do anything wrong, and you don't deserve to be punished for the rest of your life because you have a really great batting stroke to right field. The only way out is to get out of here, right now."

She still didn't move. Rain pattered down on her shoulders and ball cap. She stood under it, shaking her head.

"Maybe Eli is right," Ethan said. "Anyway, I'm not hanging around. I wasn't doing anything except taking a lead off second base. I'm going home and I won't say anything about this, and if you have a brain in your head, you'll come with me." Ethan gathered his glove and bat, and mounted his bike.

"I can't," Emily murmured, hand over her mouth.

In the distance, a siren stuttered to life.

Ethan dropped his head. He put his foot on the pedal but couldn't push it, not with Emily standing there in the rain.

"Now or never," he said. "What are you going to do?"

If you think Emily should fess up, turn to page 192.

If you think Emily should run for it, turn to page 111.

"I'm fine," Emily said again.

Mom kept her eyes on Emily but said nothing. She put the car back in gear and began to roll down the street when the phone rang. Her finger wavered over the answer button, then pulled back.

"You aren't going to answer it?" Emily said.

"Not if you have more to say."

"I don't. You can go ahead."

Mom punched the button. "Hello."

"Ms. Tuttle, this is Detective Godstein. If you have a moment, I have something to discuss with you."

Mom glanced at Emily. Emily refused to meet her eyes. "What would that be, Detective?"

A short pause. "I'd rather show you. Will you be at home soon?" His voice filled the car ominously.

"We will be there in a few minutes. Would you like to meet us there?"

"That would be fine." She hung up.

"Any guesses as to what that's about?"

Emily shook her head. She didn't trust herself to speak.

The police black-and-white was there, parked by the curb, when they pulled up. Emily opened her door and stepped into the late afternoon sunshine.

"I need a shower," she told her mother, and stomped up the stairs into the house.

The policeman waited until the Tuttles were inside before approaching the door. He rang the bell and waited.

Mom went to the door and let him in. "This way, Detective. I think you remember."

Emily heard him come in before she started the shower running. It might be the last few minutes she had to herself for a while, so she took her time in the shower. But no matter how long she stayed there, she was never going to be clean—either from the chicken grease or her greasy soul.

The policeman was still there when she came out into the family room, her hair pulled back, still wet. He stood when she entered.

"Emily, right?" he said, and tried a smile.

She didn't return it. "That's right. What's this about?"

In response, he held out a baseball. She knew right away which one it was.

"We found this at the church," he said.

Emily swallowed. "I've been looking for that. Where did you find it? In the parking lot?"

"No," he said, his voice steady, noncommittal. "It was inside the church. This is the ball that went through the window." He pointed to a pair of initials written in pen along the stitching. "ET," they read.

"Yes, those are my initials. Well, my brother's, too. It's my ball. We usually use my ball when we play over there."

The detective shifted his feet. This clearly wasn't what he'd expected to have happen. "So you admit this is your ball."

"Of course," Emily said, looking to her mother for support. "Like I said, we usually use my ball when we play. I've lost dozens over there."

The detective also shot a glance at Mrs. Tuttle. "It's the opinion of the investigators that this ball was the one that broke the window. It's got your initials on it. That looks suspicious, you have to admit."

Emily raised her eyebrows. "So, you think because my ball is there that I did this? How? I was on the field, a long way away, when the window got broken. If some kids got hold of one of my lost balls and threw it through the window, I don't see how that's my fault."

"Emily—" Mom began.

"No, Mom. This is stupid. I didn't do anything. This ball proves nothing. All it is is a fishing expedition to see if I'll confess to something I didn't do. Well, I'm not confessing, so they can just find someone else, somebody who actually broke the window, if they want to get a confession."

And Emily left the room. She took the baseball.

When she got to her room, she rolled the ball under her bed and threw herself on top of it, face down. Unfortunately, she thought, she wouldn't actually smother.

It seemed like a long time before Mom came in, as Emily had known she would. "That was quite the performance downstairs," Mom said.

"I wasn't performing," Emily said. Her voice came out muffled because her face was still pressed into the mattress.

"He wasn't there to accuse you. He just wanted to know what happened."

"I've already told him what happened. I don't know anything more. My ball in the church doesn't prove anything."

Mom sat down on the bed and put her hand on Emily's back. "No," she said, "It doesn't. And I don't know anything more than what you tell me. I just hate to see you burning up with something you can't get off your chest."

Emily rolled over and sat up. The smell of her comforter stayed in her nostrils, that familiar smell of her own bed. "Here's my chest, mom. Right here. There's nothing on it. I really hope they catch the people who broke the window, but they can stop coming here and asking me about it. I'm tired of being treated like a suspect for playing baseball."

"Then stop acting like a suspect."

Emily's mouth dropped open. "Wha—"

"You're moping about like you have something to confess. You're not yourself. I know you, girl. You're one of my favorite people. But you've been a stranger this last week or so. Something's clearly wrong and I wish you'd tell me what it is."

Emily folded her arms over her chest. "I'd tell you if there was something. But there isn't. I'm fine."

Mom sighed heavily and laid a hand on Emily's shoulder. "Okay. If that's what you want to say, then okay. But you're going back to work. You can't mope around here all day."

"Fine."

"Fine."

"Okay," Emily said brightly, huge smile flashing out.

Mom cocked an eyebrow, "Just like that?"

"Just like that," Emily said. "You want me to be happy. You want me to be my old self. Okay, here's my old self. I promise to be happy from now on."

"That might be the creepiest thing I've ever seen you do," Mom said. "And that's saying something. This is almost an Ethan level of creepiness."

"Heavens," Emily said, "an Ethan level of creepiness. Well, perhaps I had better dial it back a little."

Mom gave a chuckle. It seemed to Emily that she might actually be buying off on this. *We'll see if it lasts.*

Mom said, "I need to go get dinner ready."

"Can I help?" Emily said.

"Wow," Mom said. "Apparently this is a real thing."

"It is," Emily said. "I'm sorry I've been acting a little off. I was really stressed about the window thing. I don't like to be accused of stuff. I didn't want people to think I was a bad kid."

"No one who knows you could think you were a bad kid," Mom said, "you're one of the two best children I've ever had."

"Ha, ha," said Emily. "What's for dinner?"

The best Emily could do was be almost good enough. She flew around the house doing chores, making herself useful and working the best she could to try to get mom to leave her alone. It did seem to work. Mom relaxed around her and stopped shooting her quizzical glances. She stopped investigating everything Emily did and analyzing everything she said. It did actually seem like things were more or less back to normal.

Emily kept the pretense up long enough that for a moment she forgot she was pretending and began to feel like her old self. However, there was a round ball of shame in the pit of her stomach that simply refused to dissolve.

The next day she went back to work and did her job the best she could. She even chatted with some of the other workers here and there in an attempt to feel more like she was a part of the team. If she was going to have to be there, she might as well make the best of it. The best of it seemed to include being focused on the job but not too focused: able to churn out the fries and the chicken when those were called for, but willing and able to kick back with the employees when that opportunity presented itself. Carla had no problems with her work. In fact, she went out of her way to compliment Emily.

Mom picked her up at the end of her shift. When Emily hopped brightly into the car and chattered about how much fun she had had, mom loosened right up.

"In a day or two," Emily thought, "we won't have to go through the charade." It was, at its core, a charade. Whenever Emily had a moment to herself, her sullen mood returned.

The ball of shame surged up and threatened to overwhelm her four days into her new working life. It was Sunday. The Chicken Shack was closed on Sundays—"for religious reasons," Carla said—but Emily was pretty sure it was the religious convictions of the customers, not Carla.

Marcus, one of the other employees, agreed that it was just virtue signaling. "You don't believe in God?" Emily said.

"Yeah, I believe God exists. I just don't think he cares very much whether a chicken restaurant is open on Sundays."

Emily laughed. She had to admit that sounded plausible. It was kind of an obscure thing for God to be worried about.

"No, I'm pretty sure that it's not the religious convictions of the owners that keeps us closed on Sunday. I mean think about it. We don't cost very much on an hourly basis. The company makes enough profit off of selling one bucket of chicken to pay my hourly wage and one more would pay yours. If there's three or four of us on duty on Sunday, all they need to sell is four or five buckets of chicken an hour to make a profit."

Emily frowned, but Marcus' math seemed to work out.

Marcus continued, "The problem is, they're not going to sell three or four buckets of chicken an hour on Sunday. I used to work over a Mac burger, and we'd be lucky if we had three customers an hour all day long. There were a few more around dinnertime, of course, but for the most part, people just stayed away from the restaurants. I think that's what's happening here, too."

"They know that they will lose money having to pay people if they can't sell chicken, and selling a sandwich here and there is not going to do the job. They need to sell buckets, so it wouldn't be worth taking the chance," Emily said. "I mean they're not losing very much money anyway. Maybe a few dollars an hour. What if by staying open, people get the idea. Word gets around and they're able to stay open longer and make more money."

"It could happen," Marcus said, flipping a chicken patty on the grill. He pointed at Emily's station. "Your buzzer is about to go off," he said. She heavily gloved her hand and got ready to pull the basket out of the hot oil.

"It's like this," Marcus said. "Yes, they potentially lose a little bit of money by having the restaurant closed on Sunday, but if they can virtuously trumpet their religiosity by telling everybody that they're closed for religious convictions, then people feel more comfortable eating here. Some people even feel like it's a religious duty."

Emily furrowed her brow. "But what if it's true? What if they really do have religious convictions that prevent them being open on Sunday?"

Marcus scoffed. "Believe that if you want. Personally, I'm pretty sure that it all comes back to the money."

"Kind of a cynical attitude," Emily said. And then the lunch rush was on them and there was no more time to talk for an hour or so. During the hour when Emily was pulling endless basket after endless basket of chicken out of the fryer, she had time to think about it. What if the signaling was true? Even if it was, would her family make an eating decision based on such a thing?

She had to admit they probably would. They liked to go to small shops and companies that spent time in the community and did things for the neighborhood. Maybe those companies really wanted to be out picking up trash along the highway or maybe they didn't. Either way the highways got cleaned and the Tuttles thought it was a good idea to support businesses that gave something to the community in addition to their business product, whatever that was. Would the same thing hold true for supporting a religious reason?

Emily believed in God herself. Did she feel more comfortable supporting businesses that were run by people who also believed in God? She wasn't sure exactly. She hadn't been used to making decisions on that basis, not having had a lot of occasions to go out to eat or to choose where to shop. She certainly thought that it wouldn't hurt to support a business like that. Maybe even if the people who ran the business were not themselves terribly religious, she thought that it would probably send a signal to them that religion was important to the community. Maybe that signal would be received commercially and personally. There was no way to sort it out.

Still it seemed to make sense for businesses to appear to be religious. And for religious customers to support businesses that operated on that basis. When the rush eased and she had a chance to breathe again, she sat down next to Marcus in the back and handed him a wet towel.

"Thanks," he said. "It was a hot one today."

"It's a hot one every day," she replied.

She continued, "I've been thinking about what you said, and I agree. There is no way to know for sure if the business owners are actually virtuous or if they're just pretending to be virtuous. What would the world be like if everyone pretended to be virtuous?"

"It would be a world full of hypocrites," Marcus said.

Emily shook her head. "That's what I thought, too. But it's not true. Pretending to treat people kindly is the same as treating people kindly, isn't it? I mean, how do you pretend to take care of somebody without taking care of them."

"People do it all the time," Marcus said. "You can't tell me you haven't seen it on the news."

"No, that's not what I'm talking about," Emily said. "You would be able to fool people outside the situation, but you couldn't fool people inside the situation. In other words, a business could pretend to be virtuous without actually being virtuous. The first people who would notice would be the customers who care about the virtue of the business. It wouldn't work."

"I don't understand what you're saying," Marcus said. "Maybe I spent too much time over that hot grill."

"Okay," Emily said, "let's try it this way. Let's say I'm a business and I want you to shop at my store. You care about the St. Patrick's Shamrocks baseball team."

"Excellent guess," Marcus said. "You saw my keychain hanging from my pocket."

"Yes," Emily said, "I did. So you're a Shamrocks supporter. In order to get your business, I'm going to put a big Shamrocks poster in my front window, and on game day I'm going to play the broadcast of the Shamrocks baseball game over my intercom system."

"All right," Marcus said.

"You'll probably come shop there, even if I don't care about the Shamrocks at all, and I'm just doing it to get your business."

"Well, sure, Marcus said. "I mean, after all, you are supporting the Shamrocks by listening to their broadcast and by putting their poster up in your front window, right?"

Emily said, "In other words, what you're saying is, I'm supporting the Shamrocks by pretending to support the Shamrocks. There isn't any difference between actually rooting for them and pretending to root for them."

Marcus pursed his lips. "Somewhere it sounds like there's something wrong with that, but I can't figure out what it is."

"You can't figure out what it is because there isn't anything wrong with it," Emily said. "You're inside the situation. Now, suppose as a business owner I tell everybody else that I'm a supporter of the Shamrocks, but in my heart I actually support the Red Birds."

"That is a hypocrisy," Marcus said.

"Yes, but my behavior says that I'm actually supporting the team."

"You can't pretend to support the team without actually supporting the team. Someone will know."

"The people who care will see me supporting the team. Therefore, I support the team."

"I don't know," Marcus said, "this is getting pretty deep."

"I know," Emily said. "I'm having trouble sorting it out myself, but it seems to me that you could fool people who you were not doing business with. For instance, you could tell everyone that you were supporting the Shamrocks by donating money to them without actually donating the money."

"Yes," said Marcus, "that's the hypocrisy I was talking about."

"That might fool some of your customers, but it wouldn't fool the Shamrocks. If your customers come to your business because they see you are closed on Sunday, and you tell them you're closed on Sunday because it's a religious principle, they might believe you. Or they might not. Either way, you are supporting the religion by being closed on Sunday."

"I see it," Marcus said. "You can fool some of the people all of the time and all of the people some of the time, but you can never fool your customers because they can see clearly what it is that you're doing."

"Bingo," Emily said. "It's like trying to fool God. You can't actually do that. If you go to church but you don't really believe in Him, He knows."

Marcus nodded. "And if I really want to be open on Sunday, but I'm not open on Sunday because I think it's going to make me more money, He's not going to be fooled by that either."

"That's exactly right," Emily said. "But remember, you're not trying to fool God. You're trying to communicate something to your customers. Whether you mean to be righteous in your heart or you're just acting as if you're righteous, the people who care about your righteousness are the ones who pay closer attention."

"As long as you are engaging in that behavior, they will support you, and as soon as you stop, they won't.

I get you," Marcus said, "and anyway, I'm glad they're closed on Sunday, because I could use the day off."

"So can I," said Emily.

Marcus clocked out and waved at her. He said he would see her on Monday. Emily smiled and thought about the next day. It had never been a question before whether she was going to go to church, but now she found it might be a very difficult decision indeed.

She got home a little later than usual that afternoon. Mom said she had some errands to run and dropped her off at the front door. Emily trudged up the stairs, changed out of her damp clothes, and took a shower. She had put on what were probably going to end up being her pajamas when there was a soft knock at her door.

"Come in," she said. She already knew who it would be. Ethan cracked the door open and stood there as she sat on her bed, leafing through a book trying to find the place where she'd left off reading.

"You okay?" Ethan asked.

"I'm fine. Why do you ask?"

"Because I don't think you're fine. I know you've done a great job of acting like yourself, but I still feel like you're acting."

"I had a conversation about this at work today. We came to the conclusion that if you act like yourself, then you are yourself. You can't actually avoid becoming whatever it is you act like."

"Interesting," Ethan said. "Then I guess I have become a concerned older brother."

"You're older by, like, three minutes," she said, rolling her eyes.

"That is irrelevant," he said. "Older is older. It's a binary kind of thing. You either are or you aren't."

"Well, the fact that you are seems to me to be irrelevant to this conversation."

"I'm not sure it is irrelevant to this conversation," Ethan said, "assuming for the moment that we both know what this conversation is about."

"I thought it was about how I'm not behaving like myself, Emily replied.

"Go back and review," Ethan said. "It's about how you are behaving like yourself, but I don't think you actually are yourself."

She looked up from her book and regarded him steadily through her lashes. "This has been a long day for me, and this conversation is making my brain hurt."

"I'm sorry, he said. "I'm sorry about the whole thing. I don't have any idea what to do to help you. It's gotten a little late to go and do the confession thing, and yet I think that part of you believes there's some seriously unfinished business when it comes to that stained glass window."

"Last I heard," Emily said, "the window was getting pretty close to being finished again. I don't think there is anymore for us to discuss about that."

"That depends," Ethan said. "What kind of person you believe Emily Tuttle is?"

"Emily Tuttle has a job," she said. "Emily Tuttle comes home every night and is tired. Emily Tuttle is squirreling money away for her entrepreneurship fund or possibly to buy a car or whatever it is that comes up. Emily Tuttle started the summer as a baseball player. This Emily Tuttle thinks she has probably outgrown that."

Ethan nodded heavily. "Yeah. I thought you would probably say that. Beyond all that, who is Emily Tuttle?"

"I don't know what you mean," she said. But she did.

"Is Emily Tuttle a good person?" Ethan said.

"Yes," she said. "Emily Tuttle is a good person."

"And to Emily Tuttle, what does being a good person mean?"

Emily put her book down with its pages splayed open, knowing she would be creasing the spine. *What does he want?*

She said, "Is there some way I can help you?"

"No," he said, "I don't think so. But I was hoping there would be some way I can help you."

"I don't need any help."

"Your brother begs to differ."

"All right," Emily said, flopping back on the bed with her hands behind her head and staring up at the ceiling. "What help do you think I need? Go ahead. I've assumed the psychoanalysis position."

"Well, after thinking about all this for me, I think you need to decide what kind of person you want to be."

"Didn't we just go through this?" Emily said.

"We did, but I still don't think you've done the work to figure it out."

"And you have? You know what kind of person I want to be?"

"No," Ethan said. "I know what kind of person I'd like you to be. I know what kind of person I would like to be, but I don't know what kind of person *you'd* like to be."

Emily didn't say anything. She just stared at the ceiling. "It's pretty simple, actually," Ethan said. "We get opportunities. We make choices. And that determines the kind of person we become."

"I thought the kind of person we were determined what choices we make."

"That's also true," Ethan said. "It's kind of a cycle."

"And what kind of choices do you think I should be making?" she asked.

"You should be making the kinds of choices that will lead you to become the kind of person you want to be."

Emily said, "This is too complicated for me."

"I don't think that's true," Ethan replied. "You've always been way ahead of me on stuff like this. It's just that I think you forgot. So let me remind you that your choices are going to end up determining the kind of person you will become. It's like that story about the wolf."

"I know the one you mean," Emily said. "We hear it from grandpa all the time."

"That's right," he said. "So you know whichever wolf becomes stronger is the one you're going to feed. I don't know why but I feel like you have some really critical decisions to make right now. And I feel like whichever wolf you feed with your decisions is going to have a big impact on who you become. I just don't want to see you eaten up by the big bad one," he said, "that's all."

"Is that really all, Grandpa?" she said. "Maybe I'm not Little Red Riding Hood. Maybe I'm the Woodsman."

"You could be the Woodsman if you decided to be," Ethan said. "But one of the things about the Woodsman is he can tell when Little Red Riding Hood is in trouble."

"So?" she said.

"In order to do that," Ethan said, "it seems to me that you have to be able to tell when something's going on outside of you. You have to be aware of what's happening with other people."

"I can do that," Emily said.

"Of course you can," he said. "Everybody can. The question is whether you'll do it or not. And right now I think you're really busy trying to figure out how big the eyes are and what big teeth the wolf has."

"And what are you doing?" Emily said, accusingly.

"I'm just reaching for my axe," he said as he closed the door, and he was gone.

She lay there in bed and thought. The Woodsman comes and saves Red Riding Hood, but what happens if Red Riding Hood *is the wolf*?

The next day mom knocked on her door. "It's eight thirty," she said. "Church starts in half an hour."

"I don't know if I'm coming," Emily said, steeling herself for Mom's inevitable response.

But Mom only said, "I was afraid you were going to say that."

Emily thought for sure there'd be a lecture coming along behind it, or a reminder that their family always goes to church, or that it was a family activity, or something like that. Instead there was silence. Emily didn't even know whether Mom was still standing outside the door. It appeared she had decided to allow Emily to make this decision herself. Emily's first reaction to that was a sense of freedom. She actually was going to be allowed to make the decision. And the second sense was something closer to terror, because for the first time she could make the wrong one. There was no one around to stop her.

If you think Emily should go to church, turn to page 62.

If you think she shouldn't, turn to page 181.

The last group was easily the worst set of golfers Emily had seen. They sprayed balls all over the green, most of them not terribly close to the pin. They putted like they were trying to miss, as if it were a competition to see who could put their ball farthest from the hole and take the largest number of strokes to get it in.

And they laughed. The whole time. Everything they did was hysterical. To them, anyway.

Goofer, of course, joined right in. He would laugh at anything, that man. He called out to them, mocking their game, and they shot right back that he was the sort of guy that belonged in their foursome, if anyone did. Goofer laughed and agreed with them.

When they reached the tee, most of the other groups had finished. Their carts streamed by on the way back to the clubhouse. They called out insults as they passed, and the group laughed, which seemed their standard response to everything.

Goofer explained the nature of the rubber ducks.

"I don't think it's worth our paying money to get free strokes, Goof. It's not like it's going to make any difference."

"Yeah, too bad you weren't on hole nine. Carter biffed one so hard it almost holed out two fairways over."

More laughter. Finally one of the men—Carter, it appeared—said he'd take a swing. He forked over the cash. Emily could see there was a lot more in his wallet where that came from. Who was this guy?

Carter teed up his duck, very seriously, as if it were a shot at the Masters. His friends were already driving balls up the fairway.

"Come on, Carter. You're not going to make it anyway. We need your huge drive to scare off the pigeons."

Carter swung, a pretty thing to Emily's eye, and the duck tumbled directly onto the target in the middle of the pond.

He turned circles as if waving to a massive crowd.

Goofer's eyes seemed wedged open to their maximum. "Holy barbecued saints," he said. "Heck, everyone gets a free ball for that shot!"

The group cheered and rushed Carter in mock celebration. The bank was steep. Carter stumbled and took someone backward with him.

Each of them staggered down the bank, unable to stop. Splash.

Emily eventually retrieved the duck and, for a minute, thought she was going to have to retrieve the men, too, because they were laughing so hard they couldn't swim. Fortunately, the pond was only about six feet deep, and they could bob down and push off. They were already wet, so they spent a minute searching for drowned golf balls, until one of them lost a shoe, which Emily had to try and find, since she knew the pond pretty well by then.

She found it and tossed it up on the bank. Amid hysterical laughter and the wringing out of socks and other clothing items, the group finally made it down toward the hole and left Goofer and Emily there. Nickel's cart whirred toward them, chasing the last groups off the course. This was the moment to leave.

"Emily, my waterlogged mermaid, will you help an old man scoop these ducks back into their nest?" Goofer said. He bent down to get a duck and staggered, putting his hand to his head.

Emily reached out for him, but he had caught himself and straightened. He smiled, with just the hint of a wince. "Whoa! Must be the old man is me!"

Nickel jumped out of his cart and ran over to his father. "Take it easy, Dad. You have to be careful."

"Could be I should have taken a swim with those other fellas. It's hotter than a sauna out here."

Nickel handed him a drink with ice still clinging to the side of it. "Drink this, Dad." To Emily, he said, "Has he been drinking much today?"

"Liquor? I don't think so. Unless he spiked his own lemonade."

Goofer stopped drinking and looked at her in surprise. "Was that a joke, Miss Mermaid?"

"I meant it to be sarcastic. Did I miss?"

Goofer and Nickel laughed, short but heartily. "Well, wonders never cease," Goofer said. "Let that be a lesson to you, my boy. I rub off on everyone, eventually."

"Is that a warning?" Nickel said, scooping up ducks.

"The promise of coming happiness, son."

But Nickel's face was clouded. There was something going on here. Something behind this gaiety and jolliness.

Suddenly, it seemed to Emily very important that she find out what it was.

"Goofer, go sit in the cart with your drink," Emily said, shouldering her way in between the two men and into the midst of the ducks. "We can handle this. The ducks are tired and won't try too hard to escape."

Nickel tossed a duck into the pond. "Except that one."

"Which you're going to get yourself, buster. I've already mucked up that water forty times today."

"Forty-one is a magic number."

Emily stepped toward the water. She grabbed a stray duck and held it out. "Hold this one for me."

When he reached out for it, she grabbed his wrist and hauled. He overbalanced and the two of them hit the water together.

What with shenanigans of one kind and another, they were by far the last of the volunteers to arrive at the clubhouse. Emily made sure to ride with Nickel, hoping she'd be able to pry from him the secret of his father. But there was never a moment. Nickel and Goofer treated the run in toward the clubhouse like the Daytona 500. She finally had to get into the spirit of it, cheering madly as they raced side by side up the first fairway, whooping like madmen.

Goofer claimed to have won by a nose. The decision was hotly protested by the dripping opponents.

Mom stood there in front of the main doors with an incredulous smile on her face. "What on earth... I thought Emily would be wet, but Nickel, what happened to you?"

Nickel's face was studiously blank. "I must have slipped."

"Slipped nothing," Emily said. "I dragged him. He was seeing things, hallucinating ducks everywhere. The only treatment was to plunge him into cool water, stat."

Goofer bowed before Mom. "I must say to you, my lady, that your fair daughter is a hard worker, a good companion, and possessed of a violent and wicked sense of humor. It was a pleasure to work with her today."

Mom's astonishment was evident to Emily, however Mom tried to hide it. "Well, great. That's... That's really good to hear. So, you became friends, then?"

"He's being nice. I was a pill. But we did have a chance to discuss taxation and the economics of charitable giving, so there's that," Emily said.

"Will you all accompany me to my table for lunch?" Goofer said, bowing low as a good lord should.

Emily finally got Nickel far enough away that over the din of the gathering she could ask him the question. "What's wrong with your dad?"

"My dad? He's just a nutball. I mean, a lovable nut-ball, but still. You hung out with him all day. You know what I'm talking about."

"But that's not what I'm talking about. I know about the weirdness—he introduces himself as Goofer, it's not exactly a secret—but what's with the head?"

Nickel glanced over, then back to the assemblage, as they wove their way through the tables to the empty one toward the back. "Nothing. He just gets dizzy sometimes."

But Emily was sure he was lying. She could tell he had not had any serious training in how to deceive people. She could also tell, though, that he wasn't going to give up whatever the secret was. She kind of admired that—the loyalty to family and all. But Mom would know.

The lunch was surprisingly interesting and fun. Emily had prepared to eat and bolt—she *was* hungry—but once she had decided to have fun with things—when did she decide to do that, anyway?—it was surprisingly easy to enjoy herself. Goofer laughed and catcalled everyone, and no one minded, because he was easily the most popular person there. He was kind and good to everyone. When he teased them, they could tell it was his way of saying that he cared about them, and he was usually fairly witty—although also as corny as a Reuben sandwich—so it was easy to laugh along with everyone.

She saw how Goofer knitted the group together, how he made friends with everyone, remembered their names. And also how, when he thought no one was looking, his face took on a very different cast, almost as if all the life and color left it, and then all of a sudden it was back, and he was his old self again.

The Rotary Club voted Emily the Mermaid of the Year for her part in the proceedings, and to get the award she had to make a noise like a porpoise. It could have been the most humiliating moment of her life, but she got through it and they gave her a standing ovation complete with various animal noises, from sea and air and land.

Weird, weird people. But the good-heartedness in the room almost made her want to cry. They had raised almost $35,000 for people they'd never met, were never going to meet. And they were just giving it to them, care of the Rotary Club of Spoonerville.

When the last of the meal was cleared off and the ducks handed out ("We do not want a couple hundred rubber ducks in our garage," Mom was at pains to say), and the last of the guests seen to their cars, Emily slumped into a chair and Mom sat with her. She looked tired. They both did.

"I look worse," Emily said, looking over.

Mom laughed. "I hope so. You look like a resuscitated rat."

"What's wrong with Goofer?"

Mom got very quiet, and her lip trembled. "I was actually hoping you'd ask that." But then she didn't say anything more for a while.

Finally she sat forward and leaned her elbows on the tablecloth. "You have to understand. He's always been such a great man. He's funny, quirky, and he loves everyone. You saw." She checked that Emily had, and went on. "He's also been hugely successful in business, partly because everyone wants to do business with him. He's practically built this club from scratch into one of the most popular and successful in the state. He'd have been District Governor this next year. But then he found out he wouldn't be here next year."

"Where's he going?" Emily said, a feeling in the pit of her stomach that she hoped didn't mean what she thought it did.

"He'll be dead," Mom said. "He has an inoperable brain tumor. Six months, maybe fewer. He won't do chemo. 'It's going to kill me; I'm not giving it any help,' he says, and maybe that's the right way to go. Anyway, he found out about it a month or so ago. It's still not affecting him much—"

"But you can see it if you're paying attention," Emily finished. Mom nodded. "I want to help him," Emily said.

Mom sighed a little and reached out to take her hand. "How perfectly beautifully my plan has come together," she said.

Emily became, first, Goofer's sidekick, then his helper, then his nurse. It wasn't until that point that she realized she had also become his friend.

An endless parade of people came to see him, near the end. She helped keep the hordes at bay and let him rest. Nickel was there a lot as well, but he had work, and another pair of hands was necessary a lot of the time. "Mom's been gone for years," Nickel said. "I think one of Dad's worst regrets is that he didn't have more kids."

"You were enough for him," Emily said, because this was not a thing to tease about.

"Maybe," Nickel said.

But Goofer said as much, many times. He and Emily had long talks when there were no visitors, while the hospice staff bustled about doing medical things that Emily couldn't do.

Finally, she told him about the window.

She hadn't meant to, but they were talking, and she asked him how he always stayed so happy, even when things were, you know, like this, and he said the secret was that he gave all his problems to God. "I never held anything back. I never tried to hide stuff from Him, and when I screwed up, which was quite often, I always went right to the person I messed up with and begged them to forgive me." He tapped his shoulders. "Keeps the weight off. Then it's easy to smile."

"I don't think it's as easy as you do," Emily said.

He put his hand on her arm. "Maybe you should drop that sack of rocks, then. It seems awfully heavy."

So she told him. She started slow, and then it all came out in a rush. He just listened. Sometimes he would close his eyes, as if what she told him gave him pain, but he listened and she knew he cared.

At the end of the story, she said, tears trickling down her face, "I don't know how to make it right."

"But you want to."

"Oh. Yes. Yes, I do," she said. "I want to be like you."

"There are better people to be than me, but let's just start with what we have. You know what you have to do. You have to go to the people you harmed and make it right with them."

"I can't. And they have a new window by now, anyway."

"You can. Just ask them what you have to do. Tell them how sorry you are. Probably you should tell your folks first, and take them with you. But they'll tell you what you need to do. Then go and do it. It's the only way."

"But," she said, searching his face for hope, "what if I can't do what they ask?"

"Ah," Goofer said. "Don't worry about that. One thing is for sure: you can do it if you want to. Think of the benefits. No regrets. No secrets. Just light and peace. That's what all our goal in life should be. Make it yours."

It took a few days to get with the church people, and they called in the police, but just so they could wrap up the case. They gave Emily a stiff, stiff bill—over $20,000—which is what they said it cost to replace the window.

"But it could have been worse," Dad said, though he said it with a grimace. "They could have demanded a lot more."

"Or pressed charges," Ethan said. "Don't forget that."

"Not that this absolves you, young man," Mom said. "I think a lot of this bill is going to come from your pocket as well."

Ethan's mouth dropped open. "Wha'? I didn't do anything. I was on second base."

"You were playing. We're not going to penalize Emily just because she's a better hitter than any of you," Dad said.

"There goes my game system," Ethan said. He shot Emily a dark look, but Emily let it roll right off. She owed $20,000 to some people who didn't like her. And she'd never felt better.

Goofer's funeral was packed to the rafters. There couldn't have been ten people in town who weren't there. Everyone was sobbing—and laughing—their way through the oddest farewell she'd ever seen.

Of course, Goofer made a video for his own funeral. "I've always been told that the one thing you can't do in life is speak at your own funeral. Well, *take this, haters!*" it began, and went on from there. At one point, he mentioned Emily. "I'll be watching you and working for you, sweet, darling girl. You're going to do great things."

Emily didn't hear much after that.

Two days later a letter arrived in the mail. Right away, she recognized the crooked scrawl and knew it had to have been written right at the last. It was even postmarked the day *after* his death. Typical Goofer. If anyone could come back from the dead just to send a letter, it was him.

She slit it open with a paring knife, being careful not to damage anything inside, but she needn't have worried. The note was short, on a 3x5 card, attached to another, longer slip of paper.

Emily-

You can't sail into great things if you're dragging an anchor. Let me lift this burden for you, as a partial thank you for making the last part of my life the very best.

—Goofer

She turned over the attached slip.
It was a receipt from Our Lady Church. Paid in full.
Emily had thought she was all cried out.
Turned out, she was wrong.

The End

Her phone in hand, she stalked back to the reference desk and set the book on her table. She leafed to the first year's budget numbers, arrayed at the beginning of a chapter entitled "Founding of Malantown." It was odd that there weren't any tallies for the budgetary totals. On one side were the numbers for the expenditures, the money the city used to pay for services and goods. On the other side were the numbers for the receipts, the money the city took in through taxes and fees. Each column was sorted by category, with totals at the bottom. But they weren't in a spreadsheet, and they hadn't attempted to reconcile them. The receipts totalled a little more than the expenses. Emily made a note in her book.

She flipped to chapter two, which again began with budget figures and went on to discuss the glorious, unbroken upward path of the noble city, led by the visionary founders. Again, there was no tally of the figures, and again, the income was a little more than the expenditures. She made another note.

The third year was more of the same. Both the income and the expenditures increased, roughly together.

Wait.

She checked her notes. No. Not roughly together. *Exactly* together.

Her pulse pounded. She looked up after a half hour, as if seeing where she was for the first time. Her brow furrowed as she began to do some math.

The first year Malantown existed, there was a budget surplus of $11,448.

The second year, there was again a budget surplus. Of $12,020.

Third year? $12,621.

Rising surpluses. Not rising very much, though. Did it keep going?

The answer was yes. Year four had a surplus of $13,252, and year five $13,914. Small increases. Nothing spectacular or even interesting about that.

But year six, the trend reversed. That year brought another surplus, but it was smaller than the year before, $13,218. Then years seven through ten had rising surpluses again.

Year eleven's surplus was much larger than the others. Emily rubbed her eyes and thought. *What was unusual about that?*

Nothing, that's what. The town's just being very smart with its money, just like it says in the book. I mean, the surplus the second year is only about, what, 7% more than the first year?

No, it's about 5%, she thought. Closer to five. She brought out her phone and punched in the numbers. She stared at the result for thirty seconds or so.

It wasn't about 5%. It was *exactly* 5%.

44

Nothing terribly weird about that. It's a funny thing about accounting: you think you're never going to get round numbers, but in fact you're just as likely to get those as any others. Year two will be different.

Year two, however, was not much different. She could tell just by looking at it.

She hit the calculator and it spat out a number. She sucked in a breath.

Five percent. Exactly.

She could feel her heart pound, and looked up at the reference desk as if the man there would be able to hear it. He had gone somewhere. No one else was around.

Year three? Five percent. Year four and year five, also 5%.

What's the deal with year six? she thought. But then she saw it.

They had deducted 5%.

She laughed right out loud. No wonder the book didn't provide a reconciliation. Someone would have been bound to see it.

It was clever, actually, because looking at the raw numbers, they didn't appear to be cooked. The increases were differing amounts every year, as one would have expected them to be. It was only if you ran them down and did the math on them that they gave up their secrets.

Year eleven was weird—maybe they were worried about getting caught. She wouldn't have... *Oh. Yes.* She didn't even have to put the calculator on this one.

They just added 10% to the total, she thought. *It's the same number, every time.*

The city was baking their books. At least, they were doing it in the public release.

This was certainly worth bringing to Uncle Ben's attention, but there was always the possibility—not a very good one, but a possibility—that the numbers just seemed to work out that way. There wasn't any way to check them against anything real.

She could only keep going through the rest of the years and see if the numbers continued to tally.

It took her the better part of an hour to go through the twenty-seven years in the book. That left four more to get to the present.

Emily waited until the reference gnome came back and placed the book back on its pedestal. "I'd like the budget figures for the last couple years, please. The ones that come after that book was published."

Again the tiny smirk from the librarian. What did that mean? He reached under the desk and brought out a well-worn paperback, bound in staples. "This year's figures are not yet out. They will be—"

"Don't tell me. Slightly higher than last year's."

And what kind of reaction was that? She expected an eye roll or some sign of exasperation with the little girl who thought she was so smart. What happened instead was almost a flinch. The gnarled librarian drew back slightly, as if he scented something foul.

"I believe so, but you would have to go to City Hall for the exact numbers." His voice was steady enough, though tinged strongly with distaste.

"Thank you," she said, attempting meekness. She carried the book back to her table, conscious of the eyes on her from the nearby desk.

To her complete lack of surprise, the final three years showed precisely the same pattern as all the years before.

Emily stuffed her notes into her backpack. Ethan arrived a couple moments later, looking haggard and not terribly satisfied.

"You didn't get on much, I take it?" Emily said.

"Not much, no. The history of this town is more boring than watching grass grow. In the winter."

Emily started off in the direction of the doors. "What history were you reading? The real one, or the one the city puts out about itself?"

"There wasn't much of a selection. I got all the books there were; but, one, there weren't many, and, two, the best ones were obviously run past the ruling elite here before they saw print."

"Mine was published by the Malantown Chamber of Commerce." Emily pushed open the great glass doors and was assaulted by so much heat and humidity that it felt like stepping into an oven. "But there were still interesting things in it, if you looked closely enough."

Ethan raised an eyebrow. When Emily said nothing, he raised them both. She smirked by way of reply.

He dug in his pocket and came up with $20. "This is our money to get home," he said. "If you want to be in the vehicle when it leaves, give me some details."

"You can see it better if I list it out," Emily said, once they were safely in Uncle Ben's office. She stepped to the big whiteboard and erased a one-foot section, picked up a marker and wrote. A row of figures descended the board in a numerical downpour. She capped the marker and pointed. "Okay. This first number is the budget surplus for Malantown in its first year of operation, I mean, the first year it was separate from Spoonerville." She checked to see that Ethan and Uncle Ben were following her explanation. "All the way down, you can see there is a surplus every year."

"That's unusual, but it might just be good management," Ethan said.

Uncle Ben coughed, but followed it by saying, "Theoretically, yes. But I already knew Malantown runs a surplus every year. It isn't a very big one, as your figures show."

Emily smiled like a cat with a bowl of cream. "It's not very big, is it? Just looking at it, how big would you say it was?"

"A few hundred dollars," Ethan said. "What? Why the cloak-and-dagger?"

"And the next year?" Emily said, pointing.

"About the same. A few dollars more."

She kept pointing to the next year, and the next one, and the next. Uncle Ben frowned. "You have something here. I just can't see what it is."

"I wouldn't have seen it if I hadn't been really bored and pretty sure I was wasting your time and your money," Emily said. "But I really didn't want to come back with nothing after you offered us this job. Plus I need the money badly."

Ethan said, grumpily, "You going to tell us, or are you just making us guess for your own annoying pleasure?"

Uncle Ben chuckled. "Will we get it, if we take enough time?"

"You will," Emily said. "In fact, you'll probably get it in just a minute. I'll give you a hint. Don't look at the differences as raw numbers. Look at them—"

"As percentages," Ethan said, his voice filled with wonder. "It's 5%, isn't it?"

"Yes," Emily said.

"The first year, and the second, and the third, and..."

"Holy cats," Uncle Ben said. "It's staring us in the face. I suppose there's something equally strange about year six? Oh, I see it. It's a five percent reduction, right?"

"Right."

Ethan stood up and pointed at the eleventh year. "That's ten percent more. Did they get bored or something?"

"I don't know. What happened in year eleven? You did the history."

Uncle Ben smiled so big his face almost disappeared behind his teeth. "This is good stuff, Em. Blockbuster stuff."

"You can use this in the broadcast, I take it."

"I can indeed. I would feel like I was doing the town a disservice if I didn't." He turned back to the numbers and started muttering to himself, making notes on a pad. "Okay. I can't come straight at it—it will be better to do it the way she did, bring it up, show the numbers, let the people decide what they mean..."

Ethan jerked his head toward the door. Emily followed him out, with Uncle Ben hardly noticing they were moving at all.

"Good work, Em, I have to admit," Ethan said. "You nailed it." He scuffed the floor with his shoe.

"You did as much work as I did. You just weren't working in the same area I was. Mine had more to find."

"Did it?" Ethan said, pulling out his notebook. "You asked me what happened in the eleventh year. Interestingly, there was something. That was the year the city made a bid for a baseball tournament."

Emily did a double take. "A baseball tournament?"

Ethan smiled. "Thought you'd like that. Same thing we have this year. That's one reason the revenue had to increase by less. People wouldn't believe that revenue kept going up when the city spent so much trying to get the International Baseball Association to put the tournament here."

"Didn't work, though, did it?" Emily said, passing the reception desk and heading out onto the sweltering street.

Ethan shook his head, shrugging into the humidity and letting the door close behind him. He shaded his eyes. "They went with the Dominican Republic. But apparently the city never gave up on the idea, because here we are again."

"And this time they're going all out. New stadiums, everything."

"Wanna bet the city revenue keeps going up, even so?" Ethan said with a wicked grin.

"Not when we get finished with them, it won't!"

Uncle Ben's broadcast went live, shot right in front of the crater that was to be the foundation of a new ballpark, just one week before the IBA was going to visit the town to see the bid.

Emily and Ethan stood off-camera, working light levels and sound. But it was a great show. Uncle Ben had never been so animated presenting, but he didn't oversell the numbers, just laid them out there for everyone to see. It was obvious something shady was going on in the accounting, even if you didn't have any kind of numerical or accounting background. He finished with, "And this year, we're repeating the same folly again. The administration must have concluded that they got away with it the first time, so why not try again? But did they, citizens of Malantown? Did they get away with it? You decide."

They cut and wrapped and went to Danny's Diner for a celebration. Two months of hard work had produced something they were all proud of.

"Do you think it will get them to stop their bid?" Emily said.

Uncle Ben chewed a fry. "I don't know. If it doesn't, it won't be our fault. We did all we could."

"Would it be so bad, though, to put all that money into fixing things up?" Ethan said. "I mean, after all, most of the places they were going to put the stadiums were not very attractive anyway. Nobody likes those parts of town."

"Except maybe the people that live there," Emily said. She bit into a roast beef sandwich. "They seem to like it enough to make their homes there."

"That's kind of the point," Uncle Ben said. "Everything is relative. Yes, beautiful stadiums show off the city, but do they really bring revenue to the town? Do they help lower taxes? Do they contribute to the city's general health?"

"It seems like they do."

"It does seem like it, which is why a lot of cities do that kind of thing. But think about what happens when you knock down buildings, especially ones that were perfectly habitable. Is that a good thing?"

Emily thought for a second. "If they're going to build something else, it might be. I mean, someone has to build those new buildings, right? And that gives those people jobs."

Uncle Ben smiled. "It does. Did those people have jobs already?"

"Sometimes."

"And what happens to the work those people were going to be doing?"

"It… Well, it has to wait."

"Yes. It does." Uncle Ben reached over and took Emily's shake. He took the top off and tipped it sideways so that the shake started running out onto the table.

"Hey!" she said.

"But we can just buy another shake," Uncle Ben said. "Won't that be better?"

"No!" Emily said. "I already have a shake. If you want to buy another shake, great, but let me keep that one."

"Yeah," Ethan said. "If you want to buy a shake, you can give it to me, and then I'll have one, too. But I'd rather have more of these fries."

"But I thought it was a good thing that we get rid of this shake, so we can buy a new one. That way the shake-maker dude can have something to do."

"He's already doing something," Ethan said. "And he could do something else, like make my fries. Then Emily would have a shake, and I would have fries, instead of just Emily with her shake. Which, let me point out, she's already eaten half of."

Emily stared sadly at the half-dollar-size puddle of shake on the table. "There's a little less than half left, now."

Uncle Ben handed the shake back and rooted around in his pocket. "Or we could talk about the stained-glass window you guys broke. The stained-glass glazier has work now, and he didn't have it before. You have work and you didn't before."

"Yeah, but all my money goes to something I wouldn't have had to pay for if Emily wasn't such a good hitter," Ethan said. "I'm running just to stay in place, just to put things back the way they were before."

"Instead of moving ahead," Emily said, spooning out some strawberry goodness. "I get it. If they didn't bulldoze the office buildings and houses, the city would have both those and a new ballpark, instead of just a new ballpark. Building the new stadium looks like progress, but it isn't. It's just moving money from one bucket to another."

"Which is what it looks like they've been doing all along," Uncle Ben said, coming up with a $5 bill. He handed it to Ethan. "Fries," he said. "And a small straw-berry shake."

"Right away," Ethan said.

Emily spun slowly in place, taking in the church around her. She stopped facing the stained-glass window, bright and new, catching the afternoon rays of the sun. If it was any different from the old one, she couldn't tell.

Father MacGillivray came in from his office and smiled when he saw her. "Ah, Emily," he said. "This is a big day."

Emily couldn't quite bring herself to smile. It had been a long haul, getting the money together. She'd had very little free time, and all her earnings had gone to take care of the damage she'd caused by being exceptionally

awesome for half a second. She reached into her handbag and withdrew an envelope, white, sealed, and thick.

The Father nodded at it. "Perhaps it would be best if we did this in here," he said, indicating his office door.

"I'd rather we didn't, Father," Emily said. "Somehow it seems more fitting to do it where I can see the window."

The Father turned and paused a moment, facing the bright window. "You know," he said softly, "No matter how long I'm here, I never get tired of looking at it. It's part history, part magic. I don't know how to describe it. But more than one lost soul has been turned to God by the beauty of that lovely piece of art. It's as good as new now, and even a little better, I think."

Emily wasn't as impressed. It was pretty, all right, but she couldn't separate the beauty of the window from what it had cost her to replace it.

"Here," she said. "This should be the last of it."

The Father tore himself away from the shining mural and reached out his hand for the envelope. "I thank you, from the bottom of my heart. You did a noble thing, Emily Tuttle. Few people would have, in your place. It shows great character."

Emily thought her great character would have benefited more from having $16,000 in the bank, but she didn't say so. Only $8000 was hers, anyway. Ethan wouldn't even come down for the last payment, he was so disgusted by the whole thing.

She was ready to turn and go, but Father MacGillivray reached out his hand again. "If I may, I have two things to show you. Will you come with me?"

Emily nodded, a shade reluctantly. The Father led her through his office and around to the sacristy, right underneath the window. Now, to see it well, they had to look straight up. The sacristy smelled of old books, with the faint tang of cinnamon. Emily had long thought that if God had a smell, this would be it.

"When I had the replacement done," the Father said, "I wanted it to be exactly as it was before. But the glazier kept telling me he couldn't get the pieces to fit right. Day after day he worked on it, and no matter how he ground the glass, it didn't go into the space correctly. There was always a gap. Finally, I went to the altar and prayed." He glanced at Emily. "I do that, sometimes."

She nodded at him to continue. He cleared his throat. "That was when I knew the window couldn't be put back the same way. It had been altered and that alteration needed to be part of the window, not replaced as if it had never been." He pointed to a spot where a clean, sky-blue panel, about the size of his fist, lay nested next to another piece in green that seemed to have something embedded in it.

"Right there," he said. "That was the problem. I told the glazier what to put there, and the next day he came in and said the window was finished. It went perfectly in the missing spot. Do you see what's in that green panel?"

She squinted. It was very bright. Just then, a cloud passed in front of the sun and dimmed it, and she could see what it was.

"It's a baseball," she said, almost whispering.

The Father's smile beamed out. "It is. And there's a letter on it."

Now Emily was smiling and her throat got tight. "Is it an 'E?'" she said.

"What other letter could go there? Now you'll be embedded in this window for all time."

"Or until someone else hits a long line drive," Emily said.

The Father chuckled. "Not likely. Kids have been playing on that field for decades, and you're the first to even get close. Now, there is one other matter, if you'll come to the office."

Emily had to keep her eyes on the window—her part of the window—as long as possible, but finally she couldn't crane her neck back far enough and passed through the door into the Father's office.

He stood behind his desk, with a notebook open in front of him.

"We had a meeting of the congregation's elders last week. They made it known that they were very impressed with the discipline and honesty you and your brother have shown. They wanted me to convey that to you personally."

"I'm glad," Emily said, and she was, though it was a painful reminder of what she'd been through.

"More, however, they took a vote on establishing a new program here at Our Lady—one I feel sure you'll be interested in." He slid the notebook across the desk.

She took the rough leather cover in her hand and saw the last entry. "Scholarship fund," it said. "$16,000, approved unanimously." Emily looked up at the Father. "I don't understand," she said.

Father MacGillivray smiled kindly, like a father does at a favorite child. "We felt that the money you had paid was sacred, and we couldn't use it for just any purpose. We felt that it should be used to encourage character and learning on the part of young people, and that the first young people it should be used for were you and your brother."

Emily had to set the book down. Her hands shook.

"Accordingly, we have established the Tuttle Twins Scholarship fund, which will award money for educational and entrepreneurial activity to worthy teens in our community. The first disbursement will be $8,000, to be split evenly between the two namesakes of the fund. You, Emily, and your brother Ethan."

Four thousand dollars. She hadn't lost all the money after all.

She looked behind her for a chair. "Yes," the Father said. "By all means, sit. And if I may, perhaps I could ask you to call your brother and parents to come down for a few minutes."

Emily pulled her phone out of her pants and hit speed dial. "I think they'll find a minute," she said.

THE END

Emily was still sitting on the bed when Mom came back in to check on her.

"Preacher's pretty inclusive, but I don't know that pajamas are the appropriate thing to wear to service."

Emily didn't move. She couldn't make herself do anything at all.

"That's a 'not going to church,' is it?" Mom said.

Emily's mouth opened and she was about to say something, when Dad passed by the door.

Over Mom's head, he said, "Em, get clothes on." That was all. He didn't even slow down, just pronounced his order and moved along toward the top of the stairs. But it was enough.

Emily dragged herself to her feet and went to her closet. "I'll be ready in a minute."

It didn't take a minute in the end. She just threw a sack dress over her pajamas, pulled them off from underneath, and found some peep-toe shoes. She didn't bounce down the stairs, but there was a little more life in her step when she got to the bottom.

"Good," Mom said. Emily realized she was relieved. "Dad and Ethan are in the car already."

Emily sat next to her brother in his white shirt and tie. His shoes were polished.

They were nearly there when Dad cleared his throat a little and began to speak. "When I was a kid, about your age, maybe a little younger, I didn't want to go to church. I told my mother I wasn't going, and I made up some excuse about meeting a friend at the park, or something. I expected my dad to blow up like a bomb, because I knew church was pretty important to him, but he didn't say anything. He even drove me over to the park, where there was of course no friend. We sat there while the clock ticked on the old Buick's dash, and he didn't say anything for a long time. I spent about ten minutes marinating in my shame for having lied, and then being caught in it, and still Dad didn't say anything. Finally he said, 'I guess your friend isn't coming. Maybe he has better parents than you do.'"

Mom reached over and put her hand on Dad's shoulder. He went on. "So I felt like I had to say something, and I said, 'Nobody has better parents than me.' And he said, 'Maybe so. All I know is we're the only ones you have or are ever going to have. And I want you to come to church.' That was enough for me to say, 'But Dad, it's so boring and I never learn anything, and I just don't wanna go anymore.' He nodded and said, 'I know how you feel, son. I feel like that sometimes, too,' which was kind of like him confessing to murder, I was so shocked. Anyway, then he said, 'But I know people who keep their word, and those who don't. I know people who decided to behave a certain way, and others who didn't make that decision. Every time, the people who stuck to who they were are better people.'"

Ethan just couldn't help himself. "But Dad, you can be a good person and not go to church."

Dad laughed, just one bark. "That's definitely true. But you can't be a good person and not go to church if you know you should be going to church. You have to act like the person you are, or you can get twisted and broken. So no, Ethan, there are people who don't have to go to church to be a good person, but I think *you* have to go to church to be a good person, because *you* know there's a God, and you know He wants you there." He glanced in the rearview to see if Ethan got it. He had. Emily could see it all over his face. Then Dad's eyes slid over to her.

"That's what my dad was trying to tell me. He was the sort who went to church. He just was. So on Sunday, he got up and he went. Maybe he could have been just as good a man if he'd gone to the gym instead, but he knew that going to church made him a better man, so he went. And that's why I go. It makes me a better man—"

"You can say that again," Mom cut in.

"It makes me a better man," he said, saying it again. "Doing what I think is right makes me better, and for me, that's going to worship God. You can do what you want, and we can't make you, but you'll never be happy unless you're doing what you know is right. And sometimes you need a little push when you get stuck."

Emily was lost in thought, letting the arguments mull around in her head. They pulled to a stop in the parking lot of the church building. Ethan got out, and mom on her side. Just as Dad reached for the door handle, Emily said, "Thanks for the push, Dad."

He turned his head back and flashed her his brightest smile. Then he nodded and got out.

Of course, church was torture. The sermon was the most boring Emily could ever remember. Something about the vision of Ezekiel, and a wheel, or a ladder, or something, and how sometimes we get messages from God that we can't understand, but that didn't make them worthless. "You never know when you might come to understand what He's saying to you, and it could be something truly miraculous."

What would be miraculous would be if the church caught on fire so they could get out of there.

But she stayed. Because that was who she was.

And by the time the services were over, she was glad she came. Her friend Marian sat with her during Sunday School and jabbered away with her. Emily couldn't remember why she hadn't thought of Marian when she was deciding whether to come.

What else am I? Emily thought. *What else do I need to do to show what kind of person I am?*

I'm a worker. I like to work and I'm good at it.

She went back to work on Monday with a little more spring in her step. Marcus grabbed her on break. "I'm going to be leaving here soon," he said, checking over his shoulder to make sure he wasn't overheard.

"You got another job?"

"Not yet, but I will. It's with this guy in my neighborhood who installs windows. He's hiring a couple people to go around and drum up leads for him. I'm pretty sure I can get you an interview, too, if you want. Then we could work together."

Emily toed the vinyl tile under her sneakers. "Does it pay well?"

"A lot better than this place."

Emily shrugged. "Maybe I'll interview. Let me know if you get the job."

They exchanged numbers and the next day Marcus wasn't there for his shift. Carla wiped sweat from her brow and apologized to the staff. "I'm sorry we're all going to have to do extra work today, because we don't have quite enough people. I thought Marcus would be here. He didn't say anything different. Then I got him on the phone, and he said he wouldn't be coming back. He's got another job. So everyone just do your best, and we'll get through it."

Carla came up to Emily on a lull in the customer group. "Did Marcus say anything to you about getting another job?"

Emily thought about how to answer that. She didn't want to get in trouble, but she also didn't really want to be the kind of person who just skated on her commitments. It was wrong. She didn't owe Marcus anything. "Yes, he talked to me. I didn't know he was going to bail on us, though."

"Did he talk to you about a job?" Carla said, her voice soft.

Emily said, "He did. It sounds like a pretty good job. But I won't take it without letting you know what's going on."

"I appreciate that. I know the Chicken Shack isn't the coolest place in town to work—definitely not in the summer—but I had a feeling I could count on you to stick with it."

"That's who I am," Emily said and realized it was true.

Carla flashed her a smile. "Can you get here early tomorrow?"

"I don't see why not. But the rush doesn't start until after I get here."

"Not talking about the rush. I want to train you for other things. I can get anyone to stand over the fryer. You're too good for that."

"Well, yeah. I guess. Half an hour?"

"Make it an hour?"

"Okay. I'll talk to my mom, but I'm pretty sure it's good."

And there was more money in it, too. Carla boosted her by fifty cents an hour, which doesn't sound like much, but over 30 hours, it was the same as getting two free hours of money a week. Not terrible.

Marcus called the next week. "It's all lined up," he said. "The boss wants to talk to you. I talked you up pretty big, said you were the smartest person I'd ever worked with."

"I got promoted at the Shack," Emily said.

He laughed. "What's that worth? Fifty cents more an hour? Do you know how much I made last week here?"

"It's not all about the money," Emily said, but it was a lame comment and she knew it.

"What are you working for if it's not about money? You're not saving Guatemalan orphans." He seemed nonplussed by Emily's tepid reaction. "Listen, if you're not interested, I can take this job to someone else. There are other people out there that know a good thing when they hear it."

"No, I'm interested," Emily said. What could an interview hurt, anyway? "When does the boss want me to come in?"

They set a time for two days later, in the morning before Emily went to work at the Shack.

"I can come get you," Marcus said.

"No, that's okay. I'll have Mom bring me. She'll have to wait around anyway to take me to work after."

"But if you get the job you can bail on that place. You won't need them any more."

"I have a shift. They're expecting me."

Marcus laughed so hard he choked. "You really are the squarest. Okay, suit yourself. But I think the boss is going to want you to start right away. It probably won't go over too well that you're splitting loyalties."

Emily thought about that for the next two days. On her way out the door the day before the interview, she told Carla she was going to talk to the other company.

Carla looked up from her mop. She paused, leaning on the handle. "So that's it, then?"

"No. I'll be here for my shift."

"Even if they give you a fancy job at twice the money?"

Emily shrugged. "I said I'd be here. I have a shift to take. I'll stay as long as you need me. And I might not even get the job."

It was Carla's turn to laugh. "Yeah, and flying monkeys may come and carry me off to be the prisoner of the Wicked Witch of the East."

"West. The East Witch was killed when a house dropped on her."

"Whatever. They'll give you the job. And if it's a good one, take it."

Emily stared at her. "What about this job?"

"What about it? You think of this as the start of a long, prosperous career? It's something to do until summer ends and they put you back in a classroom. You're not hurting my feelings going somewhere else. Although it does mean I'll have to put Dominic on the register, and that will probably be the end of the franchise."

"Hey!" Dominic called, from back by the grill.

"Kidding!" Carla said. But she raised an eyebrow to Emily. She grinned back. "You do what's best for you. I'll understand. It's been fun having you here. You're a good worker. And fun to talk to, sometimes."

The next day, Emily walked up to the front of a store in a strip mall. The glass front reflected the street behind her. Emily pulled down her shades and tucked them into her pants pocket. She wiped her hands on her jeans. She was someone who took risks, who wasn't afraid to try something new. This was just feeding that person. She tugged the door open.

Marcus met her just inside. It was cool. Somewhere in the back, an air conditioner was working overtime. It felt great. There was a vague smell of acetone along with it, like industrial glue being applied.

The wide storefront was completely open with only a divider separating the back from the front of the space. Over against one wall, a fellow with short hair sat behind a desk, talking on the phone.

"You're a couple minutes early," Marcus said, taking her hand. "That will go over great."

Emily flushed a little, but she had forgotten how much she liked Marcus' dark eyes when they looked at her. She left her hand in his.

"Make sure you tell him you can start right away. This is a great job, and lots of people want it. You've got an in because of me, but you want to take it as fast as you can. We'll be working together. We can see a lot more of each other."

Did she want to see a lot more of him? She guessed so. But she took her hand back. It wouldn't look professional.

The fellow finished his phone call. "You must be Emily," he said, coming around the desk and shaking her hand.

"Yes, Emily Tuttle," she said.

"Sit, Emily." He pointed at a chair and went back around the desk. "I'm Frank Millner. I run this place. Marc here tells me you're the best worker in three counties."

Emily's smile was small. "I think he probably exaggerates. I don't know a lot about what you do here."

"We make windows and we install them in people's houses. Business has been a little slow lately, so I'm hiring two people to go around and ask people for their business."

"Door to door?"

"That's right. Does that bother you?"

"No. I don't think so. I've never done it, but it doesn't sound too hard."

"It's easy," Marcus said, leaning on the desk. "You won't have any trouble."

"How old are you?

"Fifteen."

He nodded, picking up a clipboard. "That's good enough. I can't work you more than 30 hours a week anyway. Will $15 an hour, plus bonuses, be enough?"

Emily's eyes got wide. "That's… Yeah. Yeah, that's good enough."

Millner's smile didn't reach his eyes, but he seemed satisfied. "I'll want you to start right away. The hot part of the season is right now, and we need all the sales we can get. You start this morning." He slid the clipboard across the desk.

Emily laid her hand on it, ran a finger around the clip. What kind of person was she? This was a lot of money—twice what she was making at the shack—but was that enough for her to bail on Carla?

If you think she shoul bail on Carla, turn to page 73.

If you think she should stick with it, turn to page 133.

It was too much money to turn down.

"Okay. I'll have to call my other job and tell them I won't be in, but I can start working right away."

"Awesome!" Marcus said. "I can take her out to the neighborhoods. I've got my car."

Millner kept his eyes on Emily for a minute. Then he straightened his shoulders and took a breath like he was clearing his head. "Fine. Teach her the ropes. Each of you work one side of the street. Stick together, I don't want anyone getting lost or assaulted or something."

That seemed to be it. Emily picked up the phone to call Carla, but couldn't bring herself to dial. What could she say, anyway? And Carla had as good as told her to take the job. She'd understand.

Emily went out to the car. Mom rolled down the window. "I got the job," Emily said.

Mom's face brightened. "That's wonderful! More money?"

"A lot more, yeah." Emily pasted a smile on. "I'm gonna start right away, though. They're giving me a ride out to the job site. I'll be home later and tell you all about it."

"You're starting right now?" Mom's face clouded again. "What about the Chicken Shack?"

"I called them. They understand. I gotta go now. I'll be home later."

Marcus chattered all the way out to the neighborhood they were going to work. "It's really easy. You just
ask people if we can come out and give them an estimate about their windows, and then sign them up. It's
simple, and we get a bonus for every appointment we
set. Then if they buy windows, we get a bigger bonus."

It sounded simple, and it was, but it was also awful.
The sun beat her brutally—she hadn't thought to wear a
hat—and she had no water. An hour in, she could hardly
speak, her throat was so dry. She had to wave Marcus
over and ask him to drive her home.

"Nah," he said. "We'll just go over to the gas station
and buy a soda. I'll pay. I have lots of money."

It wasn't a good day. Emily kept thinking about
Carla at the Shack, and how she'd bailed on her even
after she'd promised not to. What kind of person was
she? She thought she was someone who kept her word,
but she'd found out that was wrong, hadn't she? She
was, what? A word-breaker? No, a businesswoman. This
was just business.

"Are these really good windows?" one woman said
as Emily chatted with her at the door.

"Oh, yes," Emily said, trying to be enthusiastic.
"They're the best in the world. You couldn't get better
ones at any price."

The woman regarded her with skepticism. "I suppose."

"Can we schedule an appointment?"

"I guess. Why not?"

They found a time that Emily's calendar said would work, and Emily bounced down the steps to the curb. She called over to Marcus. "First appointment!"

He waved back at her, mounting the steps to another house, and gave her a thumbs-up.

But she got no more. People weren't home, and when she did catch someone, they didn't seem excited to talk to her, although Emily put all her charms to work on them. The day ended without another scheduling.

"These people are the worst," Marcus said. He'd had five schedulings himself, but said he usually did much better. "Too snooty. They don't know how lucky they have it. Someone ought to teach them some manners." The corner of his mouth twitched up, but he wouldn't say any more.

They took their paperwork back to the office, where Millner dropped the bomb on Emily that her one scheduling had called up and cancelled while they were driving back. So she had zero.

"It's just her first day," Marcus said, putting his arm protectively around her. "She's good. She'll do better. My first day was terrible, too."

Millner kept his own counsel on that, but made sure Emily would be back the next day for another four-hour shift.

But she wouldn't be back.

When she walked in the house, Mom and Dad were both there, at the top of the stairs.

"Hey," Emily said, stopping halfway up.

"Hey, Em," Dad said. "You got a minute? I think we need to talk."

Emily turned around.

"No, up here, in your room," Mom said.

That wasn't good. But what could she do? She marched dolefully up the stairs and into her room. Ethan was sitting on her bed, looking like he'd prefer to be beheaded than to have this conversation.

They'd brought in a chair, which they'd set by her closet. A suitcase sat there on the floor, filled with clothes and other items.

"Have a seat, Emily," Mom said.

"What's going on?"

"Well, let's see. Where should we start?" Dad said.

Emily stood behind the chair, unwilling to sit. Her heart clenched in her chest. Every face in the room was hard.

"The easy one is that you lied to me this morning about calling in to the Chicken Shack."

"You checked up on me?" Emily said, mouth open in indignation.

"I called," Mom said, "to apologize for my daughter's behavior and to thank them for having given you a chance in the first place. Imagine my surprise when I discovered that they had no idea you weren't coming in. Especially when you had directly told me, just a few minutes before, that you had explained this to them."

Emily opened her mouth to make some justification, but she had nothing to fill it with.

"Don't bother," Dad said. "That's, unfortunately, the least of your problems. You have also lied to the police about something far more serious."

Now Emily sat. She stared daggers at her brother, who hung his head and stared at the floor.

"Do not blame Ethan for this. He'll have his own difficulties to deal with. But after a conversation with the police earlier today, and with the application of certain threats, he has confessed his part in the breaking of the Our Lady window. I wonder if you are willing to do the same."

The black pit yawned before her. She couldn't admit it. She just couldn't. "I told you what happened."

"But your word is worth nothing, apparently. The police have your ball. They have the testimony of a certain young man who was pitching that day. We also have your brother's confession, although he has been consistent in his contention that the entire thing was an accident, and that you should not be punished for an accident."

"I shouldn't. If it was. I don't think it was," she said, but there was no steel in it. The corners of her eyes burned.

"You would not have been, had you confessed in the first place. But it's been more than a month now, and the police are of the opinion that the only explanation for the delay in confessing is that there was malice involved; that you meant to break the window."

"I didn't. I really didn't. It was someone else," Emily said, whispering.

Nobody said anything for a long time.

"Well, I can't help you," Dad said. He stood up, took a half-step forward, stopped, then took another step and put his hand on her head. "We'll be with you all the way. We'll do what we can. But it's out of our hands now."

The doorbell rang. Sighing heavily, as if his heart would break, Dad went downstairs to answer it. Blue and red lights flashed outside, a car ready to get Emily.

"Come in, officer," Dad said from below. "I'll get her."

The End

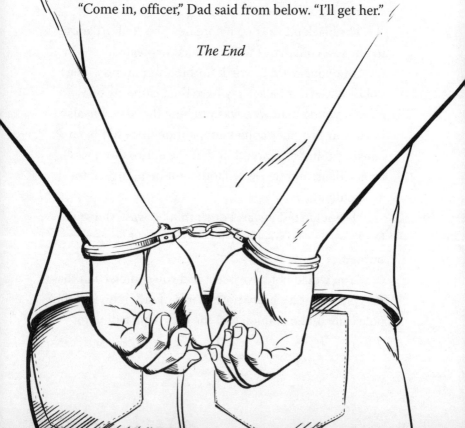

Uncle Ben studied the letter for a few minutes. "It doesn't make any sense. The best thing for the city to do, if they're going to send out something like this, is to follow through on it. Once you've delivered the bad news to people, it doesn't do any good to push the date back. It just makes people even madder."

"Shouldn't they be glad that it hasn't happened yet?" Emily said.

"Doesn't work that way," Uncle Ben said, shaking his head. "It just hangs over you and makes you crazy. But, you know, maybe we can use this."

"Use it how?"

"Well, trying to push through the city administration is like beating my head against a wall. I feel like I'm getting nowhere. And endless requests for information that keep getting stonewalled don't make compelling video. 'Our latest update is that we have no update,'" he said, mimicking his video voice.

"Yeah, that's not terribly interesting," Ethan said. "I'm not watching six minutes of that."

"We need some pressure from someplace else, something visible, something compelling. Something cool."

"A series of interviews?" Ethan said.

Uncle Ben paced. "A way to show the emotion behind all this. How people are really feeling. A way to make it personal."

"Anger," Emily said. "We need passion and pain." She looked up. "A demonstration. We need to get those people on camera and let them talk about what's happening to them. Look," she said, drawing on the white board, "on the city side we have all this hoopla about gleaming new parks, green grass, all this tourist traffic, international notoriety. Right?"

Ethan stood up and moved over to sit on the desk. "Right. So what?"

"Well, that's appealing to people. It's a benefit. And what do they lose? Nothing, or nothing that they care about. They don't like those buildings—"

"These buildings, sorry to say," Uncle Ben said.

"Okay, these buildings. But they're not attractive. Nobody that matters knows anyone that lives in any of them. They pay off the landlord, who also doesn't care, and presto, all done. No problem. But what if," Emily said, drawing on the other side of the board, "we put faces to the downside. What if we show all the things the city will lose by getting rid of the buildings here and the people who live in them? What if we make them care?"

Uncle Ben rubbed his chin. "I'm afraid some of the people down the end of the block won't exactly make the powers-that-be sad by leaving. They'll be glad to see the back of them."

"But I know someone better," Emily said, a satisfied smile on her face. "I know someone with magic powers."

"Now, just relax," Uncle Ben said. "We're going to record lots of stuff, and most of it we'll never use. I'm just going to have a conversation with you. We'll just talk, ok?"

Shiana checked with her mother. "Okay, Mam?"

"Okay," said Mrs. Douglass. "I don't think it's gonna work, but if it means we don't have to move in with your grandma, I'm willing to try anything."

Shiana perched like a splendid bird on the edge of the rust-brown couch, which had been moved so that a number of her kaleidoscopic drawings would show in a wide shot. Uncle Ben fiddled with sound levels and pronounced himself satisfied. Ethan kept the camera pointed at the little girl, zooming in just a little. Shiana glanced over and smiled shyly.

"Now, keep your eyes on me," Uncle Ben said. "Just as if we're chatting. I want to know about your paintings."

"T'ain't paintings," Shiana said, voice filled with enthusiasm. "They're drawings. Most of them is. Some I painted with Mam's paints, but I don't like those much. They're too hard to do right. The paints get everywhere."

"Will you tell me about some of them?"

"Sure!" she said, and hopped up on the couch to point. "This one here is my dog Peaches, only he's not real, because we don't have a dog."

"I see."

"This one is a bird that comes and visits me sometimes outside my window. I don't know his name because I keep trying them but he never likes any. I tried Max last time, and he flew off, so he's not Max, but he's not Baltimore either, or Happy, so I don't know what to call him."

"Maybe he'll tell you. I hear you have magic powers," Uncle Ben said, with a wink at Emily.

Shiana beamed. "That's right. I forgot. I'll just ask him next time. Except," she said, face losing all its light, "I don't know if there's gonna be a next time because we have to leave and go to someplace he won't be able to find us."

"Why do you have to leave?"

"Some bad men are going to knock down my house."

"Why are they doing that?"

She thought for a second. "I don't know. Maybe they don't like us. Except I don't even know them."

"If they met you, do you think they'd like you?"

"Sure they would. Mam says I could make the devil my best friend. I don't think the preacher would like that, but I think Mam is funny."

Uncle Ben laughed. He chatted with Shiana for another ten minutes or so, the little girl getting more and more talkative all the time. Finally he turned to Emily and said, "That's about enough, I think. I completely agree with you about Shiana. She definitely has magic powers. I am convinced she is the most charming person in Malantown. Not that that's a high bar to get over."

Emily and Ethan began packing away the equipment. Uncle Ben shook hands with Mrs. Douglass and thanked her for her help. "The next bit is going to be trickier, I think. We really need to show people what living here is like, how the neighborhood gets along."

Mrs. Douglass thought a moment. "I might be able to do something about that. Those kids have moms, too. I don't know about the boys out there putting the ball in the hoop all day every day, but I know their mamas. Let me see what I can do."

The footage was beautiful. Smiling, waving children of all ages sitting on the stoops of their three-story apartment complexes, soaking up summer sunshine, and lamenting how they were all going to be homeless and sad if the city knocked down their houses. Their mothers, inside their immaculate front rooms, wept at the displacement of their precious children from their ancestral homes. A city van, probably unsuspectingly, drove down the street. At first, there was a discussion about surrounding it and screaming and yelling, but in the end, they decided it would be far more effective to line the street and silently simply turn their backs.

The cut-together scene, complete with fade-out on the soundtrack, at just that moment, was priceless.

And viral.

Uncle Ben flipped around his laptop. "Look at this. That's 120,000 more views than there were just a couple hours ago. We blew past my most-watched episode in four hours. We'll have a million views in less than three days. I can't believe it."

"The question is, though, will it have any impact on the city? I'm not sure they're big YouTube watchers," Ethan said. He tapped out something on his own laptop and said, "But the comments... dang. Those are fantastic. 'I hope the bloodsuckers in City Hall don't think we're not watching. Kick these people out, or we'll burn the city down around you.'" He swallowed. "Well, that one is maybe a little over the top, but still. If that doesn't get their attention, nothing will."

"Emily's idea certainly crushed it," Uncle Ben said. "Even if we don't get anything else, my blog and my channel are exploding in subscribership. Just this one video is going to change everything."

"But we need to get something else. We need more. This isn't enough," she said explosively, pushing off the wall and waving her arms. "Great about your blog and all, Uncle Ben. I mean that," she said, shooting him a look that said she did, "but the point was to win this thing. Fix the problem. Stop this insanity from happening."

Uncle Ben stopped refreshing for a minute and leaned back in his chair. He kept his eyes on Emily. "I thought the point was for you to get a part-time job so you could pay off a broken stained-glass window."

Emily stood still for a moment and kicked at the carpet with the toe of her shoe. "Well, it was. I mean, it is. But this is bigger than that. The new window is already getting built, and I'll pay them back somehow—"

"You'll keep this job as long as you want it, I'll tell you that."

She smiled a little. "Thank you, Uncle Ben. Really. But I just want to bust. Until the city formally abandons this idea, those people down there are on the chopping block. There's got to be more we can do to help them." She threw herself down in one of the orange plastic chairs like a sack of potatoes.

Ethan kept his eyes on the screen. "Wow, sis. You're really into this thing. You might want to calm down."

"I don't want to calm down. I want to work."

Uncle Ben clicked his pen and said, "So what do you want to do?"

Emily frowned and screwed up her face. "I wish I knew."

Ethan said, "If anyone's interested, I have an idea."

"I could use one," Emily said. "I'm even driving myself crazy here."

"My favorite YouTubers are the guys from that comedy show, you know, Studio D? They do all the crazy stuff but it's all super clean?"

"You never stop watching them," Emily said. "So what?"

"Hey. You like them too."

"Beside the point. I assume this is going somewhere?"

"Touchy, touchy. I'm getting to it. I watched their very first video a couple years ago. It wasn't very good, actually. But I kind of liked it and Mom let me, because it was clean, so I kept watching. And that's the point—there was always something to watch. They put a new video out every couple days for like two or three years."

Uncle Ben said, "That's sort of what I do."

"Right," Ethan said. "And it's what has made you pretty successful. But it's always you. These guys have different people on every sketch. Same rotating group, but new people in new sketches, playing new characters. It keeps things fresh. Plus, when you hit a gusher—remember that one they did where the guy kept getting hit by soccer balls, no matter where he went? That one was hysterical—you have more content for people to grab and share and like and stuff."

"I have that," Uncle Ben said, "but that's not going to help your sister much."

"Hang on. We now have a gusher. You have a viral video. That's going to help you, and keep us in work, which is great, but we need to go vertical with it. I gotta draw this." He got up and went to the whiteboard. "Here we have Uncle Ben's show." He drew a thick black line across the board and marked twenty or so ticks on it. "Each one of these is a show, okay? But then we get this." He blocked one of them so that it looked like a whole rest in a piece of music. "There's our viral hit. It's going to feed traffic back along this line to all the other stuff. But we can use it as a platform to push something up, too, not just along." He drew a rectangle rising from the single block, like a skyscraper rising from the ground. "There's a chance to get a lot of eyeballs in this space here, as long as all those videos are about the same subject. That's called 'going vertical' in marketing speak."

"Which you got from a different podcast," Emily said.

"What if I did? That doesn't make it wrong. That podcast, by the way, does this. If you want lots of general marketing stuff, great, they have topics all over the place. But when they get a popular topic, they spend two or three episodes on it, which captures a lot more traffic and holds more interest. We can do that, too."

"Another video?" Emily said. Ethan could tell she was in, just not quite seeing it yet.

"Twenty more. Or, you know, whatever. But not with Uncle Ben. These should be videos shot by the people themselves, selfie-style. They're, I don't know, updates on the situation, personal to the people there. We're not shooting them. We just push them through our channel, linking and cross-posting them."

Uncle Ben stared at the board. "We should involve as many folks living there as we can get."

"Yep. You telling me you wouldn't watch those guys talk about their neighborhood and what they'll miss when it's gone?"

"The neighborhood kids were telling me about the epic jump-rope battles they had down at the end of the street where no cars go. Half the neighborhood comes out for those. It's like the Super Bowl," Emily said.

"That could be a lot of video," Uncle Ben said. "And we won't have control over it. Who knows what they'll say?"

Ethan shrugged. "You don't ever know what people will say. We don't have to link to videos that are crass or profane, but we could throw a lot of traffic at the ones that are on message. And they could throw some our way, too. We can work together."

"They all have phones?" Uncle Ben said.

The twins looked at him like he was crazy. "Okay, okay," he said, his hands up in defense. "Just asking."

The twins were already starting for the door. "Seriously, what century does he think this is?" Ethan said.

If the traffic for the initial video was hot, this was nuclear.

And it was clear that not only were they getting eyeballs from around the country—and the world—but people in Malantown were paying attention, too. Comments got more pointed, and some of them began showing up on the city website in the comment sections there, too. The local Gazette reported being flooded with emails and citizen video about the proposed project. None of it was supportive.

"Look at this," Ethan said, a few days later. "This video was shot two blocks over. Those houses aren't even going to be torn down. But they're talking about how the neighborhood is going to be destroyed and the rent prices driven up until no one who lives there can afford to stay. We didn't even talk to those people."

"That's how viruses work," Emily said, clicking away on some video herself, editing sections and adding music. "They don't stay in the neat little boxes you put them in. Haven't you seen epidemic movies? The disease doesn't seem too impressed by police tape."

Uncle Ben stood at the wall, facing the big calendar there. "The visit of the international baseball people is in three days. Do we want to do a special for that?"

"I do," Emily said. "I've been thinking about that for a month."

"Me, too," Ethan said, glancing over at his sister. "What's your idea?"

Emily got up and went to the whiteboard. "It goes like this," she said, drawing a pair of fat lines from the top of the board to bottom. She ranked some boxes, big and small, along either side. "The road," she pronounced, like Pharaoh giving directions for building the pyramids. "We line each side of it with people, everyone we can get. We know where the baseball people are going, don't we?"

"Not exactly," Uncle Ben said, "But we can probably work it out. They'll want to overlook the river, for sure."

"Great. Whatever they do, we make sure we send people. Not a couple people. Dozens. Hundreds. As many as we can get. Make the baseball people see us."

"Them, you mean," Uncle Ben said, but he was smiling.

"No. Us. We're all in this together. We work here," Emily said, stamping her foot on the floor, "and this building is coming down, too, so we're all part of this. We lose our jobs—"

"You would have, but now I don't think you will."

Emily glared at Uncle Ben the way she glared at Ethan. He waved at her to go on. "We lose our jobs; they lose their homes: we're all part of what happens here."

"You want shouting and waving stuff?" Ethan said.

"Nope. What I want is dead silence. No talking. No jeering or catcalls. Just a whole bunch of people standing and watching and saying nothing at all."

Uncle Ben looked at Ethan, one eyebrow cocked. "That's... creepy," Ethan said.

Emily's smile broke out like the sun on a spring day. "I'm counting on it." She capped the marker and dropped it in the tray like dropping the mic after a perfect delivery. "What's your idea?" she said.

"Thought you'd never ask," Ethan said. "I want to go the complete opposite direction. I want noise. I want chaos. I want the baseball people to never want to come anywhere near this town again."

"How are you going to pull that off?" Emily said.

"Simple. We're going to have a series of 'mechanical failures' that block the road," Ethan said, winking. "Then we're going to make them tow the vehicles while everyone in the neighborhood shouts and screams and yells at them. I want signs and loud music and dancing and screaming and the whole production. I want to get in their face and show them the anger of the neighborhood about this. And of course, I want cameras. Lots of them. Ours, theirs, news cameras, everyone. I want to see this thing from ten different angles."

"Hard to put together," Uncle Ben said. "That takes a lot of coordination."

"No more than hers does. And given the group in this neighborhood, I think it's a lot more likely we can get people to yell than that we can get them to stand silently for a couple hours, making people feel uncomfortable."

"But you have to admit they would, if she could pull it off," Uncle Ben said, considering the white board. "Well, that's a tough decision. What do you want to do?"

If you want to choose Emily's idea turn to page 253.

If you want to choose Ethan's idea, turn to page 218.

This foursome did not believe it was in contention for any prizes, so their interest in Goofer's peddling was limited. Only one fellow, a tall sandy-haired man with a slight limp, bought the chance to hit a duck into the pond.

He glanced at Emily. "Must be nice to be in the water on a hot day."

She squinted up into his face, framed by blue sky. "I guess."

He put the duck down on the grass, took his stance, and whacked it into the dead center of the target. "Yes!" he said, throwing his hands in the air.

Emily slid off her perch into the water.

He waved her back. "Nope. Thanks for your help, miss, but I've got this one." And he dove into the pond.

His friends howled and reached for their phones. "I wish I'd gotten that!" one of them said.

Goofer whacked one of them on the back. "Now that's getting into the spirit. I think all four of you have earned mulligans on this one." He handed each of them a ticket.

"Dan, you're out of your freakin' mind," his partner said, reaching down to haul his friend out of the water.

Dan jerked him off his feet and plunged him into the pond with him.

"Oh, what the heck," the other two said, exchanging a glance and a shrug. "Here, hold this," one said to Goofer, handing him his phone. The other two swan dived in to join their friends.

What an incredible waste. Who were these guys? Emily was disgusted. She had to do this, but they were doing it for fun?

Apparently. Judging by the hysterical laughter, and the mutual splashing and dunking, these guys thought this was big fun indeed. She couldn't get it.

But part of her knew that once upon a time, she would have understood. Part of her knew that the Emily from... well, before... would have thought this was hysterical. She tried to reach into herself for that feeling again, for that person. It slipped away from her. She slipped away from herself.

She had slipped much farther away from herself than she had realized.

But what of that? The Emily from before was a sucker. A rube. Naive and stupid. It was better to be who she was now.

Off in the distance, she saw Nickel's cart coming up the fairway.

"Hey, Goofer, I'm gonna go get dried off," she said, mounting the cart.

He might have said something to her, but she couldn't hear him with the wind whistling in her ears. She didn't look back.

Some of the foursomes were already in the clubhouse when she arrived. One or two of them greeted
her, thanking her for getting their ducks for them. She
attempted a bedraggled smile, which didn't make it
into full flower. The smells of lunch floated out into the
lobby. Emily's stomach growled. She wondered if she
was going to get some of that.

It took a minute to find the bathroom, during which
time she had to pass a hundred people, every one of
whom stopped what they were doing to look her over.
She knew she must look like something that crawled out
of a pond. Well, she had. Thirty or forty times.

She spent a long time in the bathroom, trying to
put her hair back together. The mess was far worse
than she'd thought. Inside like this, still wet, she began
to shiver. She sniffed and dabbed at her nose—getting
red, she thought—with a piece of tissue. Great. She was
officially a freak.

The Rotarians, however, were either all freaks
themselves or they were used to them. Celebrated them,
even. Groups poured in from all over the course, total-
ing up their scorecards and calling insults to each other.
With few exceptions, they stopped to thank her, shake
her hand. Call her "mermaid."

No, she thought. Not that.

But it was too late. Once one of the guys had
thought of that and said it out loud, she was officially
The Mermaid. Mom came by from wherever she'd been
and put her arm around Emily. "Fun day?" she said.

"If any part of this were fun, I have officially lost my mind."

"Hey, Mermaid, come get a picture with us!" one of the foursomes called from their table.

Emily wanted to crawl in a hole and disappear.

She nearly did. Mom had a place at her table for lunch, but Emily said she'd eat in the kitchen. She was more self-conscious than ever about her bathing suit. Lunch was good, except for the part where they called her out to give her a standing ovation and name her the official mascot of the tournament.

Better and better. No way could the day get any less appealing.

The kitchen had a back door. Emily used it, and stalked back to the car. At least it was warm out here. She had dried off. Maybe she could tilt the seat back and get a nap.

That didn't work, either. Too many cars coming and going, people calling out to one another. And her hair smelled like sewer. Her suit itched. No matter what she did, she couldn't get comfortable.

Maybe she dozed off a little, because when she opened her eyes next, the sun had moved a couple inches across the sky, and there were two people talking behind the car. Their voices were too low for Emily to make out what they were saying, but she could see through the back window that it was Goofer and Mom. Goofer would say something, his hands patting the air in between them, like he was calming her down. Then Mom would say something. Emily didn't have to know the words to be able to recognize the tone of voice. It was the one where Mom had had enough.

What had she done? She got up, she came with, she even did the stupid thing she got assigned, even though clearly all these people were cracked in the head, and none of what she was doing made any sense. This wasn't how she thought the day would go. Heck, it might have been better to go get a crap job someplace rather than have to put up with this.

It got quiet for a second, and Emily quite clearly heard her mother say, "I'm sorry she was such a pain."

"She wasn't," Goofer said. "She's clearly upset about something, but she did her work all day without complaining. It would have been better if she could have gotten into the spirit of the thing, but teens have it rough. Don't be too hard on her."

"Thank you," Mom said. "You always have the best attitude."

They exchanged a brief hug, and Mom opened the back. Goofer deposited a box. Mom slammed the door and came around to climb in her door. She sketched a wave to Goofer's departing back and slid into the seat.

"Good day?" she said.

Emily snorted. "I can't wait to get home and get this muck off me."

"I'm proud of you for sticking it out. It would have been nice if you'd hung around to help clean up, though. There was a lot of work to do."

"I cleaned up all day. That was my job."

Mom set her mouth in a line and put the car into drive.

"Speaking of which, I am getting paid for this, aren't I? That was the deal? Work for you or work for someone else. I take it you're paying me?"

"I would if you were worth paying. I think I have some change here in the ashtray. That's about what you were worth today."

Emily's mouth dropped open. Mom was a lot of things, but sarcastic and bitter was never one of them.

"What? Did you want me to praise you for being a brat? Goofer and Nickel, not to mention half the town, tried all they could to be friendly to you. You did nothing but mope around like a death-row convict. That's not… I don't know this Emily," Mom said. She sounded genuinely worried.

She closed her eyes just for a second at the next stop sign and bowed her head. Emily could have sworn she was praying. "I'm sorry, Em. That wasn't fair. You did come, and you did work. All day, according to Goofer. You did exactly what you were asked to do. Yes, I will pay you minimum wage for your work today. You earned that. I'm just sorry not to have had my exuberant, playful girl with me."

Emily knew Mom wanted her to look at her, so she deliberately kept her head pointed out the passenger window. "Maybe it's just not me any more. Maybe I'm growing up."

"Those people back there are the most grown up I've ever come across. And they have fabulous attitudes. They can make fun out of anything."

"Grown up? Those are big children. The last group that came by all dove into the pond. Did you see them come back to the clubhouse soaking wet?"

Mom nodded, her face solemn. "Did you see them whooping it up and laughing? That group finished dead last of all the foursomes, but nobody had a better time."

Emily was disgusted. "Is that what life is all about? Having a good time?"

"Yes."

That was it. Mom said nothing else, just kept driving.

"Yes? Life is about having a good time?" Emily was incredulous.

"It is. There are a lot of other things in it than good times, but mostly we can't do anything about those things. When they come, the hardest thing to do is to keep having a good time, but it can be done. It always makes things better."

"Probably better to just lose your mind, then. Saves time."

"You're thinking of Goofer."

"As one example, yeah."

Mom jerked the wheel to the side and pulled the car abruptly off the road. She slammed on the brake and ripped the shift into park. When she turned to Emily, her face was hard, harder than Emily had ever seen it.

"Goofer is one of the best men this town has ever seen. He is unfailingly generous with his time and his money. There are hardly any families in this community he hasn't touched with his kindness. He takes pictures of families for free. He volunteers at the elementary school, and not in the gifted classes, either. He takes the hard kids, the ones who are struggling, and he helps them see that they have worth. He's made a fortune in his business, but he's kept almost none of it. People are drawn to him because he is genuinely happy all the time, even though he's had some of the worst luck of anyone I know. Now THAT is what I call a grownup. You can't be a person like that through moping, or even through hard work. It has to happen from inside you. You have to be good. I really hoped you'd see that today."

Emily knew she shouldn't, but the words were out before she could stop herself. "It's easy to be happy when you're as rich as you say he is."

"Not when you're dying of cancer, it isn't."

Emily blinked.

"That's right, Queen Miss. Goofer probably has six months to live. Inoperable brain tumor. It's going to get him, but he's going to go out with a smile, living his life to the maximum right to the end. You might want to pack your cynical attitude back into its trunk until you know enough about life to know when to get it out and use it. Which ought to be never, but you know best."

Not another word was exchanged, all the way home.

Most days working with Mom involved weird charity events, volunteering at soup kitchens, weeding the gardens of older people who couldn't get down to do it anymore. Once in a while, she got to read and comment on things. Mom never spoke sharply to her again, but there was a freedom to their relationship that had ended that day, and it didn't come back.

Emily knew she was sour. She just didn't know how to get back the sweet. Things weren't bad, they just weren't good, and nothing she did could get the goodness back.

Our Lady church had a special service to commemorate the finishing of the new window. Mom thought it might be good to go to it. Emily didn't see how she could get out of it without arousing suspicion, so she went and sat next to Ethan. They spent the entire service not looking at each other.

"Really great about the window getting finished," Dad said on the way out. "It looks wonderful, just like the original."

That's right, Emily thought. Just like the original. Now we can be done with this. The church is happy. The case is closed. I can move on.

But she couldn't. Things didn't get better.

One day, at the end of the summer, she got a letter in the mail. It didn't have a return address. Mom handed it to her as if she knew who it was from.

"Open it," she said.

Emily took a knife from the block and slit the end of the envelope. She bounced the letter out. It was short, handwritten, in a shaky scrawl that made it hard to read.

To the Mermaid:

Spending the day with you was truly a highlight of my summer. You're in a tough spot, and you probably don't understand why an old man cares about why—trust me, I do. Whatever it is that you're carrying, lay it down. Get rid of it. The best way to do that is to tell someone. Talk through it. Don't ruin one more day lugging it around. It will blind you to all that is good in the world, and you never know how much time you have to enjoy it.

You're a great kid. Don't let anyone tell you different. And don't waste a day.

—Goofer

Emily's eyes burned. He couldn't know. He just couldn't.

"His funeral is this weekend," Mom said, pretending to leaf through the mail. "He died Monday."

The letter couldn't have been posted before that. He'd taken one of the last moments of his life to write to her.

Why?

Emily sat in the back of the hall for the funeral service, in a black dress that matched her mood. She said nothing in the car on the way, and nothing on the way home. In her fist was clutched the letter, now crumpled and here and there dotted with salt tears.

What was so important about her that he would use one of his last breaths thinking of her? Why did she mean so much to him? Emily knew she'd been curt. Had certainly given him the impression—sadly true—that she didn't like him and thought he was insane. Then he gave her this gift. Why?

Was he truly happy? What if it wasn't insanity, or just an act? What if it had all been real? How could anyone who knew he was dying be so cheerful, and work so hard to make others cheerful?

"Get rid of it," he had written. Emily wondered if that was it. He was light inside, because he wasn't carrying guilt around. He wasn't burdened with terrible things he had done. He was simply himself.

She thought about what that might be like. Then she remembered that she had been that way, once. Just for a moment she could remember the incredible freedom of not carrying secrets. The joy of it took her breath and made tears start in her eyes.

But it was too late for that. There was no way back.

The car pulled into the garage and Dad got out. Mom still sat there, head bowed.

Another spot joined the ones on the paper.

Mom reached for her door handle to let herself out.

Emily turned, and before she could stop herself, she said, "Wait."

It was a long conversation. But Goofer would have thoroughly approved.

THE END

"Rooting around in dusty old libraries isn't my idea of fun, but this is your project," Ethan said, nodding at his sister. "I'll do whatever you say."

"I say libraries are my superpower, so that's where I want to go," Emily said. She eyed Uncle Ben. "What are we looking for?"

He frowned. "I don't know, exactly. You might have to go back to the beginning, where the split happened between Spoonerville and Malantown. Up to that point, both towns had pretty similar backgrounds and pretty similar development. Then the split happened and—"

"And Malantown exploded. New ballpark, high-rise condos, business buildings," Emily said.

"While Spoonerville went nowhere," Ethan said, bitterly.

"Now, now. Let's be fair. Spoonerville has a terrific stained glass window in the sacristy of Our Lady of Lourdes," Uncle Ben said.

"*Had*," Ethan said.

"And thanks for bringing that up," Emily said.

Uncle Ben chuckled. "The library is six blocks north and four blocks east, but I don't suppose it would be a good idea to have you walk the distance. I'll have a car come get you." He tugged open a drawer and removed a file folder. "Here are my research notes up to yesterday. It's not a lot to go on, but it might give you some ideas."

He got serious for a moment. "This has to work, kids. We don't have a lot of time. If you can't come back with something good, I'm going to have to put other people on it and probably send you home. You get me? This is a big deal. It's my livelihood. I need this stuff and I'm trusting you to get it."

"Understood, Uncle Ben," Emily said. "We won't let you down."

"This is pointless. I hate research," Emily said.

"I thought libraries were your superpower." Ethan thumbed through a thick book of budget notes from the first four years of Malantown's existence. He jotted a note on a piece of paper and turned a page.

The table in front of them was crowded with books of all sizes, plus a good number of very old microfiche and some newspaper archives. It smelled heavenly, Emily had to admit.

"It's not actually libraries, it turns out," she said, running a finger over the spine of a volume. "It's books, specifically fiction, which this stuff decidedly isn't."

"Oh, I don't know," Ethan said. "I'm getting a very weird vibe from this material here that makes me wonder how much of it we can trust." He looked up and saw the look on her face. "Okay, so you don't care for this and you made a mistake. Fix it. Don't do the financial research. Look up the story of the town." He waved her away. "Go find a reference lady or something. They have them here, same as anywhere else." She left him at the table as he muttered something under his breath, clearly suggesting he was a bit irked.

The library wasn't terribly well stocked with staff, for all that it was new and beautiful. It took Emily ten minutes of searching to run down a harried gray-haired man in the young adult fiction section and tell him what she wanted.

"Good grief," he said, "No one has asked for that for years. Not in the summertime, anyway. What did you say you wanted it for?"

"To bring down the corrupt administration and lead the city's people to freedom." She thought it sounded grand, and besides, telling people the truth was awesome, especially when they didn't believe a word you said.

"Oh, well then," the man said, "I suppose I need to be in the best form to help such a noble cause. Come with me."

He abandoned his cart of books and headed off toward a mysterious part of the library that was so empty it made Emily think no one had ever been there. She hoped her benefactor/guide had brought a compass.

Back six or seven stacks rose a section of bookshelves labeled, "Rf Mlnt Beg-Secdec," whatever that meant. The guide dragged his eyes over the titles at eye level, shook his head, and crouched.

Emily crouched beside him. "What are we looking for?"

"Not looking for. Finding." He dragged a thick book off the shelf, blew the dust off the top, and handed it to her. It said *Spoonerville: A History*.

"Wrong book," Emily said. "I'm looking for books about Malantown."

"Right book," the guide said. "Remember there was no Malantown until the Great Flood."

"In Exodus?"

"No, in the valley here. Wiped out a lot of the river district." He found another, slimmer volume, executed the same procedure, and stacked it on top of the first one. Two more followed. As he moved part of the shelf to reach another book, something fell behind the stack.

"What's that one?" Emily said. She'd have pointed, but her hands were occupied.

The guide looked at her. "What one?"

"That one, there," she said, pursing her lips and trying to use them to point. She had heard about some cultures doing that, and immediately realized the disadvantages of lips versus fingers in such cases.

He did not take the hint. "I don't know what you're talking about."

"Something fell down—" she began, but never finished.

"What are you doing here?" a voice said from behind them. The guide bolted to his feet.

"She wanted to learn about the early days of Malantown," he said. Emily would have sworn he sounded guilty of something, but there was no telling what.

"Young lady," the voice said, "are you researching something for school?"

"Not exactly," Emily said. "But I am interested in something specific, yes." She stood up and found herself eye to eye with a round, short man of red face and very little hair. He wore a name tag that said "Fraggle" and "Head Librarian."

"Specifically what?" Fraggle said.

"Financial records for the first twenty years of Malantown."

His eyes narrowed. "You're in luck. Those collected records are available in a book published by the Malantown Chamber of Commerce a few years ago. It's sitting right on the main reference desk." He tilted his head sideways to read the titles of the books in her arms. "That book, along with these, should do you nicely. Come along."

He led the two of them away from Rf Mlnt Beg-Secdec and out into the main reading room, to a wide, curving desk polished to a mirror shine. There, on its own pedestal, stood the book, like a volume of sacred scripture. "The city is most excited about the bid for the baseball tournament. The representatives will be here in only a few days, and we hope to show them there is no better place for their exhibition than right here."

"It would be a wonderful thing," Emily said, feeling just a bit dazed. "I play baseball myself."

"Do you indeed?" said Fraggle, but not as if he cared. "If you'll just take one of the chairs there by the table, I can make sure you've got all you need. Thank you for your help, Reginald. I can assist her from here."

Reginald, the guide from before, vanished as if swallowed by quicksand.

At least it appeared that she would be able to find something useful; the figures she needed were right there in the book.

Emily wrote for several minutes, taking down the information, before deciding it was probably better to just take pictures of it with her cell phone. Every year there were budget figures, and yes indeed, they escalated dramatically after the split. The budget skyrocketed. But the receipts kept pace, and there was always a little bit left over. It nagged her, though. Something wasn't right.

If the figures were here, so easy to get, why didn't Uncle Ben have them?

She went back to find Ethan. His table was covered in books. "I need Uncle Ben's research notes," she said.

He didn't say anything, just pointed at the corner of the table. She leafed through the sheets inside the folder, and there, toward the back, were budget figures. She checked them against her phone. They were the same, right down to the penny.

"This is no good," Emily said. "Uncle Ben already has the research. He doesn't need me to get this stuff."

"Then we're in trouble," Ethan said, not looking up. "I'm getting some good stories here, but nothing that's going to make a podcast go viral."

Emily put the folder back and strolled to the reference area, thinking about the figures. She wandered through the stacks, past juvenile books, and into the children's section. Emily saw none of it. Her concentration was all on what was going on in her head. Something about those budget figures. What was it?

If you think they should walk around some more, turn to page 154.

If you think they should dig deeper into the figures, turn to page 43.

It might have been rain, or it might have been a saltier water dribbling down Emily's face, but something in her broke and her feet began to move. She reached out mechanically for the handlebar of her bike. Her fingers closed over the handle. But she couldn't go any farther, just stood there dripping with her eyes locked on the gaping hole in the church.

Ethan skidded up. "Come on, Em. We've got ten seconds."

She did not move.

Ethan reached out his foot and whipped it through her kickstand.

The toppling bike pulled Emily back to the present. Her eyes kept their wildness, but they were seeing things again, other things than a gap-toothed window.

The bike rolled forward. Emily swung her leg over the seat and onto the pedals. The tire gripped in the wet grass, tore some loose, dug in again. Now she was moving. Panic seized her heart and squeezed, lending power to her legs as they pumped the pedals.

She and Ethan fled down the street, away from the church, away from the sirens. Also, away from home.

They ended up in a pocket park by the waterfront. Next to them, through a screen of bulrushes and scrub, the river rolled away past, gray and indifferent. Across the river, squat buildings, built for structure and not for scenery, hunkered along the opposite bank. Emily sat like one of them, a tiny building with less hope, perhaps, than they, and let the rain fall on her.

Ethan found a hunk of cardboard in the nearby dumpster and tugged it out to use as an umbrella. He hung his mitt and after a moment, Emily's, from his belt and carried the shelter over to cover his sister. He didn't sit, just used himself as a column with a roof of sodden TV box. The rain splattered off the brown box and drizzled to the left onto the muddy grass.

Emily didn't move for a long time, long enough for the rain to give up trying to drive them off.

"You can't stay here forever," Ethan said.

"Who says? I'm sure I can find stuff to eat in the dumpster."

"I looked. Nothing there. They must have picked up recently." He shook the water off the box, and laid it to the side. "Come on, Em. It's not the end of the world. Nobody's going to tell."

She finally reacted, turning her head just enough to let one eye gaze at him through a screen of bedraggled hair. "Nobody? Really? You think Davy is going to keep his mouth shut? What about Brayden?"

"Brayden is a coward."

"Cowards talk. Plus he hates me because we won the game."

"We did win, didn't we? Oh, wait."

"Wait what?" Emily turned a bit farther.

"We didn't win. You have to circle the bases or the homer doesn't count."

She stared at him. "That's crazy."

"Baseball is like that. You have to circle the bases. It's a rule. It's why you always see the team gather at home to wait for the hero to finish running all four bases before they mob him. So we didn't win, because you didn't touch home."

"Brayden won't know that. He won't know the rule, either."

Ethan shrugged. "Not that it matters. He never liked you. He'll tattle at the first chance; you're right."

"So I have to tell. I have to go back."

Ethan kicked at the muck and twisted his hands. "Maybe Eli is right and you didn't do anything so wrong. Heck, the window broke because you did something righter than anyone has ever done it on that field. I kind of want to go measure it."

She was horror-struck. "You what?"

"I mean, yeah," he said, a little sheepishly. "It was a sweet shot. I just want to know how far you hit it."

Emily made a growl of disgust and got to her feet. She wiped her hands on her jeans and reached out for her glove. Ethan handed it to her. They carried the limp box back to the dumpster, tossed it in, and stood a moment by their bikes, looking back up the long hill.

"I have to go back," she said.

"Yeah, I guess you do. But it's not just you, it's all of us. We all did it, if you did."

Emily made a face. "You think that's how Brayden is going to tell it?"

"Well, no, probably not."

She sighed and climbed on. Water from the seat soaked through her pants and made her itch. The hill was long and darkening. No more rain fell, but the clouds lay thick and let through no light. It took far longer to climb up the hill than it had to come down it, and well before they reached the top, they knew the trouble was vast and deep and waiting for them.

Red and blue flashed on and off into the dusky sky, along with bright white spotlights, shining on the gaping hole in the church wall. Emily drew to a stop just across the street from the ballfield, behind the trunk of a huge oak tree. Only her head poked out. In the gloom, no one could see her from the church lot. Ethan pulled up beside her, breathing hard.

"Wow. I didn't know we had that many police cars in Spoonerville," he said.

Emily said nothing, just watched her doom gather. Through the fence, they could see the shapes of bodies milling about, and hear shouting, though not well enough to make out any words. Her face was ashen under the dim reflection of the lights.

The field was silent and empty. Emily couldn't believe she'd ever wanted to play baseball at all. But she kicked her stand down and crept across the street onto the field. Then, as fast as she ever had, she ran ninety feet toward the church, made a right angle, and ran ninety more. She belted around second, around third, and sprinted across the hard white mat that served as home.

Then she got on her bike and rode home.

They said nothing, either of them, to their parents. Not even when Dad said, "Coming home I saw a lot of cops gathered around Our Lady. I wonder what that was about."

Ethan didn't look at Emily. Emily didn't look at Ethan. They kept their eyes on their tuna casserole and green beans.

"How was your day, Ethan?" Dad said. "You haven't said a word all through dinner."

"It was, you know, summer. We rode bikes awhile, and I read a book—"

"Which one?"

"King Arthur," he said, mentally grabbing for something he knew was on his bedroom shelf.

"Thought you'd read that one already," Mom said. "Like, six times."

"Wow," Ethan said, playrully rolling his eyes. "My parents are so strict they'll get on me for reading a book I like several times."

"Easy, champ," Dad said, smiling, but with something in his face that said he was curious. "Nobody's getting on you. Just wanted to know. Wouldn't you like to read something you haven't read so many times that you've worn the cover off?"

"I do. I mean, I am. Anyway, that's what we did. Just a regular old lazy day in which nothing happened at all."

Emily closed her eyes. He might as well have confessed right there. But their parents didn't seem to suspect anything serious.

"Em, you don't look well. Are you okay?" Mom said and leaned over to lay the back of her hand on Emily's forehead. "You don't have a fever, I don't think, although you are a little warm."

Emily saw a glimmer of light at the end of the dark tunnel of her life. Or, maybe not at the end. More like a

tiny access lamp in the dark tunnel. Whatever. It would get her out of this meal.

"Actually, I don't feel very good. May I be excused?" she said, already standing up.

"Of course. Maybe you should just go to bed."

"I think I will," she said, taking her plate to the sink. She looked back and Ethan was scowling, but that was his own lookout. She had nothing to do with it.

She climbed the stairs and it seemed as if her mother's diagnosis was coming true all by itself—she felt achy and bone-tired. It was a great chore just to drag herself up

the stairs and to her room, where she fell over on the bed without even bothering to take her clothes off.

But sleep didn't come. She rolled over and dumped off her shoes, lying back with her hands under her head, willing her eyes to close. But they popped open on their own and wouldn't obey.

Emily took her book off her nightstand. Hundreds of pages left; Brandon Sanderson could write a doorstop of a novel, that was for sure. She tried to focus on Kaladin and Shallan and Dalinar, but she kept getting their names mixed up, and the book was so heavy. Finally she let it slide off onto the mattress. Maybe if she listened to some music.

Nothing worked. She shut off the music after the fifth song. Every one of them seemed like an indictment of her decision, reproaching her for running off instead of sticking it out and confessing. But how could she? There was no way she could pay for that window.

It really wasn't her fault, anyway. She hit the ball perfectly; that was what you were supposed to do. It wasn't her fault that the window was too close to the field. If the church had been so concerned about the window in the first place, they should have put a net up. Maybe a higher fence.

She turned toward the wall, trying to find a position that was comfortable.

Footsteps sounded on the stairs. Mom, probably, coming to check on her. The bedroom door creaked open.

"Em. Psst. I know you're not sleeping."

"Ethan, I'm sick. I'm trying to rest."

The door closed. For a moment she thought he'd gone out. But then he said, from over by her window, "I wonder if the police will come here."

"Why would they do that?"

"It's no secret who plays on that field."

"But lots of people play there. We're not the only ones."

"Only ones playing baseball, I bet. Only ones big enough to hit the ball far enough to… you know."

Emily rolled onto her back. "We aren't big enough to hit it that far, either."

"That turns out not to be true."

"Oh? I think it's definitely true. It has to be 500 feet from home to the window. Even big-leaguers can't hit the ball that far, except once in a while. So I couldn't have hit it there."

Ethan's brow furrowed. "You're not serious. We all saw it."

"Did we? I don't know what we saw. I've been thinking about it. Maybe it was just a coincidence that the window got broken the same time I hit that homer. I bet it wasn't the ball at all."

"Em, I know you don't want this to be your fault—and it's not, really—but this is a little bit weird, isn't it?"

She sat up, a look on her face Ethan had never seen before. "You know nothing about it. You didn't even see. You were on second, trying to score."

"I saw. Everyone stopped to look."

"No. I'm the only one that really had a good view. And the ball was short. It must have been some other kids playing around there, vandals or something. I'm pretty sure I saw some kids over there in the parking lot while we were playing."

Ethan stared. "You're serious about this."

"Absolutely. It wasn't my fault. I didn't do anything. I don't know how the window got broken."

For a minute Ethan just left his eyes on her defiant face, then he turned on his heel and headed for the door. "If that's the story you want to tell…"

"It's the truth. Why wouldn't I tell it? It makes more sense than me hitting a massive home run. Impossible, right?"

He opened the door and went through. When he closed it, it didn't click. Emily put her pillow over her head, and after a while, she finally went to sleep.

The police did, in fact, come.

Not right away, but the next morning about halfway to lunchtime, a black-and-white came rolling down the street and stopped in front of the Tuttle house. A plainclothes policeman got out, checked the address against a small notebook, straightened his shoulders, and climbed up the walk to the front door.

Emily saw all of this from behind the curtains of the front window. She'd been waiting, pretending to read, sometimes plunking about on the piano. If they didn't come today, they weren't going to come, so she had her eye on the front of the house.

When the doorbell rang, she started in with the practicing again, working some fast scales as if she hadn't heard anything at all.

Mom passed through the room on the way to the door. She didn't say anything, not even to reprimand Emily for not getting the door. Emily played softer, hoping to hear.

"Mrs. Tuttle?" the man said. "Detective Goldstein, from the Spoonerville police department. I wonder if I might have a word with you."

"Of course, detective," she said. "Come right in. Can I get you something to drink?"

"No, thank you," he said. Emily heard the door close. "Actually, I was wondering if your children are home."

"Ethan and Emily? They are, yes. Why? What's this about?"

He didn't answer, just came after Mom into the front room where Emily was practicing. Pretending to practice. Whatever.

"Ethan!" Mom called up the stairs. "Come down a minute."

"It won't take up much of your time," the detective said. "I just need to ask a couple of questions about yesterday."

Ethan bounded down the stairs and skidded to a stop in the front room when he saw the detective.

"Ethan?" he said.

"That's right," Ethan said, with a bright smile. He extended his hand and the detective shook it.

"And this must be Emily."

"Emily, dear, will you stop for a moment? The detective would like to ask you some questions. Although," she said to him, "I'm not sure what about."

The detective perched on the edge of the couch. "Yesterday evening someone broke the stained-glass window at the Church of Our Lady of Lourdes, just up the road. The church sits at the far end of a vacant lot where kids play baseball sometimes. I wanted to ask your children if they had been playing there yesterday, perhaps they saw something."

Emily lifted her gaze from the carpet. It seemed to weigh a thousand pounds. "Yeah, we were there," she said. "Just before it started raining. We had a game on the field with some other kids."

"And did you see anything?" the detective said. Emily couldn't tell from his face or his voice if he was fishing, or if he genuinely didn't know. She went to the story she had concocted last night.

"We finished the game right before the rain started," she said. "Right as we were leaving, I think I may have seen some kids playing in the parking lot. It's possible they had something to do with the window."

The detective's face stayed carefully neutral. Emily didn't dare look at Ethan. "Could you describe these kids?"

"I don't think so. That's really far away from where we were playing. I couldn't see them very well through the fence."

"Is it possible," the detective said, turning his face to Ethan, "that someone from your group broke the window?"

Ethan cleared his throat. "I don't, um, I don't think… We play there all the time. Like Emily said, the church is kind of far away up the right field line. We, um, our group went home when it started to rain. I don't think anyone would have broken the window on purpose."

"I didn't say they did it on purpose," the detective said, making a note. "Did you see anyone over there?"

Ethan shook his head. "I didn't. I was kind of focused on the game."

The detective stood up. "Thank you anyway. I didn't think there was much point in asking, but we're trying to round up all the leads. I appreciate your time."

He turned to go, and Emily couldn't help herself. "Mr., uh, Detective. What would happen to someone who broke that window? I mean, I'm sure it was an accident and all. The church would have insurance, wouldn't they?"

"They would," he said heavily, "but the window is beyond price. It can probably be replaced, but we would really like to find the persons responsible. If it was just an accident, then there wouldn't be any charges, but there's still the cost of the window, which now the church will have to bear by itself. If it was malicious, then that's misdemeanor vandalism. We don't want vandals running around loose in our town." He waited, his eyes on Emily like lamps. She tried to keep her face as blank as his.

Finally, he sketched a salute to Mom and excused himself. She shut the door behind him.

"That must have been what Dad was talking about at dinner last night," Mom said. Her eyes were on the door. She missed the look that passed between her children.

Mom turned back. "Did you really see some kids over by the church?"

"I think so. Yeah. I mean, it was getting dark and there were clouds and stuff, so I couldn't see all that well, but someone was over there."

"Terrible," Mom said, shaking her head. "I don't know this town any more. That's such a beautiful window. I've loved looking at it. I hope they can fix it, and they catch whoever it was that broke it." She moved off in the direction of the kitchen.

Ethan waited for her to go, then whispered, "You're going to get it, Em. They're going to figure it out."

"Figure what out? I didn't break it, I told you." Her voice was low. She didn't think Mom would be able to hear it.

"Yeah, your story is cute and all, but it's never going to hold up, because you've forgotten something important."

Emily glared daggers at him. "Oh yeah? What's that, since you're so smart."

Ethan drew back and walked toward the stairs to his room. He paused, one foot on the step, and said over his shoulder, "What happened to the baseball?"

"This window thing is a real tragedy," Dad said, riffling through the newspaper. "That stained glass has been there longer than the town. It's got to be the most valuable thing in the whole place."

"They can fix it, surely," Mom said, dishing up meat loaf.

Dad shook his head. "Nobody is sure. The damage was pretty severe. And it's not like there are stained-glass makers everywhere. You can't just go down to Stuff Mart and get some stained-glass pieces to put in the window."

Emily stirred her cocoa. "Isn't the window getting broken kind of a good thing, though? I mean, if there aren't a lot of stained-glass people around?"

"How do you mean?"

"I've been thinking about it. So there's one stained glass dude in this region, say. How many stained glass windows are there? Ten? Twenty? Are people putting in a lot more? I don't think so. So that one guy, how much business is he doing? Not very much, right?" Her face was brighter than it had been for a while.

"No, probably not very much," Dad said, putting down the paper with a neat fold. "What's your point?"

"My point is that now he'll have business. Maybe the first business in a while. He's going to get a big job, and it will take him and whoever works with him a long time to do it. He'll get paid a lot, when he wasn't making anything before. Then he'll be able to hire people and pay them, and those people will buy stuff, and it's just... It's good for everyone. It will be a good thing for the town."

Mom and Dad passed a look across the table, and Dad nodded. "You've done a lot of thinking about this."

"Yeah, I have. I mean, it's not like it's important to me, but I was just... thinking."

"Ethan, what do you think?" Mom said.

Ethan screwed up his face for a second. "What she's saying sounds right. But I can't quite see how it could be. I mean, suppose we said, 'Hey, this is great. We... I mean, someone... broke a window, and now the window guys are going to get more work.' That's a good thing. But then what if we put a gang together and went around breaking windows, so more window people would have work? That seems like a good thing, but it can't be. Can it? How can destroying things be good?"

"That's the question, all right," Dad said. "And it's a tricky one. Maybe we can use this dinner as an example and see what we can learn." He pulled the plate of meat loaf over to his side of the table. "Take this meat loaf. Is this good food?"

"The way Mom makes it? Absolutely," Ethan said.

Dad smiled, picked up the meat loaf tray, and laid it in the trash.

Ethan came halfway out of his chair. "Hey! What are you doing?"

Emily's mouth dropped open. "I didn't even get any yet."

"Don't worry about it. We can make more, right? Think about those guys that sell ground beef! Now they'll have more work, selling us more to replace what we lost."

"But Mom will have to work harder, because she had meat loaf already made and now it's gone."

"But she'll have more work. I thought that was a good thing."

Ethan frowned. "I thought so, too, but now I don't know."

"Look at it this way," Dad said. "We could eat the meat loaf we had. Instead of using more money to buy new meat, we could use that money for something else. But now we can't, because we have to use it to buy more food. Mom was going to go to the movies, but now she can't, because she has to make more food for us. And so on."

"I get it," Ethan said. "People are busy, but they would have been busy doing something else anyway."

"Em, do you see?"

"I don't know. The stained-glass people weren't working. Or, they were, but they could work harder. Because the window is broken, they'll get that work."

"True. But where is the money coming from to pay them?"

"The church."

"And what was the church going to do with that money?"

"I don't know. Probably nothing."

"The church is a non-profit. It can't keep money. It has to do something with it."

"Okay. New Bibles or something."

Dad took a drink. "Fair enough. New Bibles. Will they have new Bibles now?"

Emily went back to staring at her plate. "No," she said in a small voice.

"They will not. So Bible sellers get no business now. There are no new Bibles. With this much money, they'd probably do more than get new Bibles. Maybe they'd even give it away to the poor. But now they can't, because they're spending it on a window."

"At least they'll have a new window."

Dad went to the trash and took the plate out, with the meat loaf still on it, just as before. Mom cocked an eyebrow. "You better have kept that plate from touching anything."

"Trust me," Dad said, but he checked it over before he put it back on the table. "The church had a window. When this is over, all they'll have is the same thing they had when they started. But the money they had to use to replace it will be gone. And what they were originally going to do with that money, they won't be able to do now. There won't be any progress. Things will not get better."

Ethan took a huge slice. "That makes sense. If we go around destroying things, all we're doing is moving backward or staying in the same place. We're not making progress."

"Right," Dad said. "Otherwise, why not go around breaking windows? If it's so good for the economy, why not?"

"And why stop there?" Mom said. "Why not burn the whole church down. Then the construction guys can get more work, too." She took a slice and put it on Emily's plate.

"But it seems so logical," Emily said, picking at the tablecloth.

"It does," Dad agreed, his hand over his mouth because he was still chewing. "Lots of people believe it. You hear it all the time after natural disasters. And I guess in a world where everyone has everything he could ever want, and nothing better could ever be made or created, then breaking things would give people work to do. But I don't see that being the situation any time soon."

Mom got up and went to the oven. She twisted the dial to turn it off and got a hot pad out of the drawer. "You can understand it a lot more easily if you think of time instead of money. You want to read a book. I take the book and shred it. Can you read that book?"

"Nope," Ethan said, craning his neck to see what Mom was going to take out of the oven.

"To get to read that book, now you have to spend time finding another copy, maybe having to go to the library or buy it. It takes a lot of time to get back to where you started. That time never comes back. It's gone and you didn't do with it what you meant to."

"This applies to video game time, too," Dad said, "which we're at pains to remind you periodically. That time is gone. You can't get it back. You have to use it while you have it."

Emily picked up her fork and spit some peas on it. "But can't that be a good thing? Not the video games," she said, with a glance at Ethan, "or, yeah, Instagram, Dad, I get it, but the having to go find another book. I might come up with a better book than the one I was going to read."

Dad blew out a breath. It was a thing he did when he was thinking. After a minute, he said, "That's true. But there you're talking about making something good out of a bad situation. You can do that and you should. But does that mean we ought to go around making bad situations?"

"I guess not."

Mom set a pan of cake on the stove. "So I shouldn't dump this cake in the trash?"

"I'd request that you not do that," Ethan said.

"But you might be better off not eating it," Dad said, ruffling his hair.

"It's a risk I'll just have to take."

"As soon as you've finished your vegetables."

"Fine. I'll eat them. Then the cake will be making the best of a bad situation," Ethan said.

Emily finished her plate and even managed a slice of cake, but she wasn't up to games with the family that night and said she'd rather go read in her room.

"You're spending a lot of time up there these days. It's not like you. Are you sure you're okay?" Mom said, a hand on the stair railing. Worry lines creased her forehead.

"I'm okay, Mom, really, I am. I guess I'm just getting tired of summer."

Mom's lines deepened. "Now I know something's wrong. Fifteen summers I've known you, and never before have you been anything but devastated when summer ended."

Emily tried a smile, but it sat on her face like a wart and didn't fool anyone.

Mom was in her room at dawn, sitting in the comfy chair and reading. Emily woke up at the turn of a page.

"Wha... Mom?" Emily said, sitting up a little. "What are you doing here? Is something wrong?"

"Something is," Mom said, "But you don't seem to want to tell me what it is, so I'm here to give you a kick in the pants so we can make a little progress. Starting this morning, you have two options: go find a new job or start working on some homeschool stuff I want to test out."

"I've been doing jobs since I was nine, Mom. Do I really need to go get a new one?"

"Look, dear. You're ambitious—or at least you always were before—and there are help wanted signs all down Main Street. And as I said, you don't have to get a job, but if you don't, I have plenty of work for you to do. I bought a new homeschool curriculum, and I want to see how it goes. You're the perfect person to playtest it."

Emily rubbed at her eyes and checked her phone. 7:17. Cruel, although not that unusual. "What about Ethan?"

"What about Ethan? I don't see him moping around as if someone important has died. He's got his own stuff to do, but you need an intervention and I'm here to intervene. You get two minutes to decide, and then I'll decide for you." She closed her book with a whack and her smile was bright.

"I'll wait outside."

If you think she should go find a job, turn to page 168.

If you think she should work with Mom, turn to page 233.

Emily pushed the clipboard back across the desk. "I can't start today. I committed to a shift at my other job. They're counting on me. I can probably start the first of next week, depending on what they say. But I can't start before then." Her heart hammered in her throat and her leg trembled.

But Millner's eyes twinkled. "You're sure? There are a lot of people that want this job, you know. What am I supposed to do until you're ready? Just keep the job open?"

Marcus was appalled. "This isn't what we talked about. She's kidding," he said to Millner. "She can start right away."

"She can talk for herself, I hope," Millner said. "Or I shouldn't hire her at all."

"I'm sorry," Emily said. "I promised. I keep my word." *I do keep my word*, she realized. *Even when it's hard.* Something broken inside her snapped back into place, and she felt a warmth flood through her that had nothing to do with the summer weather.

Millner picked up the clipboard and stood. "Well, that's that, then. You realize I'll have to interview other people."

Emily stood and took his hand. One quick shake, but she could look him in the eye. "I understand. You have a business to run. If you can't find the person you want when I'm free, I'd like a chance at it again."

"No promises."

"Of course not," Emily said, knowing that was it. She'd be stuck in the Shack for the rest of her life. But her heart was light, and it seemed the world was a brighter place.

Marcus walked her to the door, fuming. "You blew a good thing here," he said. "I thought we had a deal."

"No," Emily said. "You had an idea and I didn't think it was a good one. Besides, what good is a deal if one of the people in it doesn't keep her word? I'll see you around."

"Maybe," Marcus said, and walked back into the back of the store.

Mom said, "You didn't get the job?" Emily was gratified to hear that she sounded surprised.

"They offered it to me, but I have a shift to take. I can't quit without notice. It wouldn't be fair."

Mom patted her shoulder. "That's my girl," she said. "I bet you anything that was more impressive to them than if you'd just taken the job and left your other place in the lurch."

Emily doubted that, given what had happened afterward, but it was done nonetheless. She got to the Chicken Shack ten minutes early.

Carla didn't even ask, just gazed at Emily until Emily had to say something. "I got the job."

"But you're here. You turned it down? I thought I taught you better than that."

"I didn't turn it down," Emily said, strapping on her apron. She slapped the light off in the locker room. "But they wanted me right then, and I said I already had a place I had to be."

Carla spat into the sink and turned the water on to wash it away. "You're a fool. They'll give that job to someone else."

"I'm your fool, though. For another few days at least. I'll still leave you if the job's open next week."

"I'll fire you if you don't," Carla said, consulting a list on the wall. "You're on the register. Don't steal the money."

Emily laughed right out loud. She couldn't remember the last time she'd done that.

She called Millner the first of the next week. "Mr. Millner, this is Emily Tuttle. I'm available to start the middle of this week, if the job is still open and you still want me to do it."

"Miss Tuttle," said the voice on the other end of the line. She could have sworn he sounded pleased to hear from her. "The job is no longer available. I want you to know, however, that it was with a heavy heart that I hired the incompetent, lazy brother of my sister's ex-husband. I have kept peace in my family, but I have a feeling I lost out on a much better employee."

Emily was a little disappointed, but not nearly as much as she thought she would be. "Thank you for considering me," she said, looking at Mom to make sure she was doing this right. Mom gave her a thumbs up. "I hope you'll let me apply if another job opens up."

"I'll call you if that happens. Good luck, Miss Tuttle."

And that was that.

Sort of.

A couple of weeks later, the day Carla told Emily that she was putting her in training to be a shift captain, Marcus pulled up in his rusty SUV and rang the bell. Emily let him take her out to the curb in the late afternoon sunshine. Honeysuckles had just bloomed down the street, and the scent filled the street.

Marcus' face bore a wicked smile. "You gotta see what I have here." He took her hand and led her to the back. The door swung wide. "Check this out," he said, and drew out a box with a top-of-the line gaming system, still wrapped in plastic.

"That's pretty great," Emily said, and in truth she was impressed. She knew how much one of those cost and knew Ethan had been saving up for a while to get one. He wasn't even close yet.

"Yeah. You're missing out. We're killing it out there while you slave away in that shack." He slid the box back into the cargo area. A corner snagged on a rough blanket, pulling it up and exposing the stock of some kind of gun.

"What's that?" she said, pointing.

He tugged the blanket back in place. "Secret sauce," he said. "Insurance." He slammed the door. "We're going out to the movies later. You want to come?"

For a moment, she could remember why she had liked it when he paid attention to her. But now he seemed shallow and uninteresting. A bird swooped past, chittering. She put her hand up to block the sun. "I don't think so. I'm kinda tired from work. And I don't think my mom wants me dating yet."

"This isn't a date. It's just, you know, some friends getting together." He put his hand on the side of the SUV, leaning on it, inches away from her. "You're missing out again," he said, his mouth close enough that she could smell his breath. Minty. He had great teeth.

"Could be," she said. She really could be. But she didn't want to get into that car with him. "Next time."

His mouth turned down. "Won't be a next time," he said. "That's something you're gonna learn one of these days. You gotta take your chances when they're in front of you."

He drove off. She stood on the curb and watched him go, wondering if he was right.

Three days later Dad tossed the paper to her as he sat down to dinner. "Isn't that the place you interviewed?" There was a picture of a window with three small holes in it. BB shot, she guessed. The article was about a rash of broken windows a few blocks away. Police had no leads and were blaming the destruction on vandals from across the river. They had interviewed Millner, because his business was booming, and he was the only installer in town.

"Broken windows aren't a blessing to anyone," Millner said. "I know people think it's great for us, because we get this business, but it hurts homeowners. When this started happening, I did some research. It might seem like it's good for the economy, but it's actually bad for everyone. Even us."

"Yeah," Emily said. "That's him. I'm surprised he understands the broken window issue, economically."

"Seems a pretty decent guy," Dad said, taking back the paper.

Emily thought for a second. "I think he might be." She reached out again. "Can I read the rest of that?"

The next day, after work, she asked Mom to drive her over to the window store.

"Are you going to ask for a job?" Mom said. "I thought you were happy at the Chicken Shack."

"I am happy there," Emily said. "This is about something else." But she wouldn't talk about it, no matter how much Mom pressed her.

The inside of the store was just as cool as ever. Millner seemed surprised to see her. "You look like you've been on your feet a while," he said, offering her a chair and a bottle of water.

"Thanks," she said.

"I don't have a job for you," Millner said, "not that I wouldn't like to offer you one. I hope this isn't about that."

Emily shook her head. "I wish it were. It's something a little more serious. Marcus isn't here, is he?"

"No, he's out on a job. Is this about him?"

Emily pulled the article out of her bag and handed it across the desk. "I read this. Good quote from you, I thought."

He scanned the paper. "I was really glad I'd done some research, or I could have made a fool of myself," Millner said, and looked up at her. "It's nice of you to bring this, but I already had one."

"I think I know who's breaking the windows."

Millner slowly set the paper on his desk. "That's a serious accusation."

"I know it. But I saw the BB gun in the back of Marcus' SUV. Wrapped in an old horse blanket."

Millner blew out a breath and ran a hand over the stubble on his chin. "I can't go to the police with 'this girl saw something.' They'll laugh at me. They already interviewed everyone here."

"I figured they had. But I thought you should know."

"How do you know I'm not the one ordering them to do it?"

"I don't. It's a guess. You seemed a decent fellow."

He shook his head and muttered something under his breath. Emily got up and put the empty water bottle on his desk. "Thank you," she said. "I was thirsty. And I hope I'm wrong. Marcus isn't that bad a guy."

"He's sweet on you, you know that?" Millner said. "I kind of hoped the two of you wouldn't work together, because I don't see that ending well."

"It won't even get started, I don't think," she said. "I'll see you around. Good luck."

The paper had the whole story two days later. Millner had turned in Marcus and his sister's ex-husband's brother after following them home from work and catching them shooting out the windows in a neighborhood they were going to be working door-to-door in the next day. He credited an anonymous tip for giving him the idea, and pledged that his company would be installing new windows for free in the affected houses.

Dad watched Emily read it. "Anonymous tip, it says."

"I'm not anonymous. You've known my name for fifteen years."

"I'm proud of you, Em."

She pursed her lips. "I tell the truth. It's who I am."

"There could hardly be a better thing than to be truthful."

That night, she knew what else she had to do. She was someone that told the truth. It was, indeed, who she was. She kept her word. She was honest. She was a hard worker.

And she had a confession to make.

Mom and Dad sat with her at the police station as she explained what had happened on that dark afternoon a couple of months back. She took all the blame. The police said they believed her, but the church would probably be very angry and demand that she pay them back for the cost of the window. Because she had confessed, though, they'd probably not press charges for vandalism.

"I have money saved," she said. "Not enough, for sure, but some. And I'll work for the rest. I'm not afraid of work."

The officer stood up and shook her hand. "I can see that. You're an impressive young lady. I'm very glad you owned up to this. You're going to go places."

Her picture couldn't be kept out of the paper, unfortunately, and she had to tell the story to the news more than once before it all went away. The Chicken Shack actually did better business for a couple of weeks, because people came in to meet the famous hitter that destroyed the Our Lady window with a home run that was labeled, in the paper, as "fearsome, even for a major leaguer. Surely one of the unluckiest—but most impressive—four-bag shots in local baseball history."

At about two in the afternoon, at the end of a long, long shift, she was about to close down the register when the bell over the door dingled that they had a customer.

Emily drew out her brightest smile and said, "Can I help you?" when she realized that she knew this customer. "Mr. Millner," she said. "I've never seen you eat here before."

"I'm not here to eat," he said. "I'm here to talk to your boss."

"Uh," Emily said, trying to think of what she could have done wrong that he would need to talk to Carla. "I think she's in the back."

But she wasn't. She was right behind Emily, wiping her hands on her apron.

"Clint," she said.

"Carla."

"You can't have her."

Millner reached into his pocket and drew out a roll of bills strapped with a rubber band. He popped the band off, peeled off two hundreds, and dropped them on the counter. Emily's eyes bugged.

Carla shook her head. "No."

He stripped off another one, laid it on the pile.

Carla's "no" was a lot less definite this time.

He did it again. "I can do this all day, Carla. You know me."

Carla closed her eyes. She rolled her hand over one time. He added another bill to the stack, and she sighed and reached for them.

To Emily, she said, "This man would like a bucket of chicken. Clock off and deliver it to him. He'll be in the back corner of the restaurant. You should listen to whatever it is he's going to say. When he's finished, come back and find me." She went back through to the rear of the kitchen and left Emily there with Millner.

"I'll be just a minute with your chicken, sir," she said, punching the register.

Millner never had to hire another receptionist until Emily finally quit to start her own business. He never had a salesman even close to as good as Ethan.

And Carla still got Emily on the register during the evening shifts.

The window was paid back in record time. Emily liked to go there, sometimes, and just sit in the chapel. It's especially pretty in the late afternoon, when you can hear kids playing baseball in the field with the extremely high right-field fence.

The End

Emily trudged up the sidewalk in the afternoon heat. She was sure that if she'd had an egg, she could fry it right here on the lip of a trash can.

"Don't fall behind," Ethan said. "I don't think this is the part of town you want to be alone in."

The beer-can-strewn street was choked with cars, parked and moving, most of them older and rusted, but here and there were some that were bright and shiny with extra LED lights like mobile Christmas trees. To either side of the road, the business development had given way to walk-up apartment buildings. People sat on the steps and watched the twins as if they were something from a zoo.

"Do you suppose these are the people who are losing their houses in the reconstruction?" Emily said.

"Who else?" Ethan said. He pitched his voice low and glanced out of the side of his eyes.

Emily responded by walking right up to a pair of younger kids sitting on the stoop of a house. "Do you live here?" she said.

They regarded her with wide eyes but no sign of friendliness, almost as if her words didn't mean anything to them.

"Is this your house?" Emily said, pointing to the red brick three-story behind them.

One of them, a little boy, with a streak of dirt down the left side of his face, nodded just a bit, so quickly it was hard to be sure they'd seen it at all.

"Mam!" the girl said, whipping her head around so her braids flew. "Some lady here wants to know if this is our house!"

"Why not answer her, then?" a voice yelled from inside the house.

The girl turned back to Emily. "I'm Shiana Douglass," she said. "This is my house."

"Part of it," the boy said. He pointed. "That part." The ground floor, on the right. "I'm seven," he said, as if that definitively established the truth of his words.

"I'm fifteen and my name's Emily. I think your braids are pretty."

Shiana beamed shyly, deciding they were friends now and no more needed to be said about it. "Who's that?" she said, eyes on Ethan.

"He's my brother Ethan. He's fifteen, too."

The two kids nodded. Preliminaries out of the way, they proceeded to let the twins in on everything they knew all at once. "This is our house but the city men come and say we hafta move but we don't wanna go because Mam says we like it here better than anyplace we been before."

"What city men?" Ethan said. The two kids glanced over at him, but kept their information only for Emily.

The boy said, "They come back when school was in and say we hafta move, but Mam says they can't throw us out because we ain't goin' and that's good because my best friend Amie, she lives upstairs and she hasta go too and her folk are a long ways away and we won't never see each other no more when we go. So I guess we ain't goin.'"

The twins unbent and looked in the window of the part of the house that belonged to the kids. "Can we talk to your Mam?" Ethan said.

The kids looked at Emily. "We want to ask your Mam about the city men. Maybe we can make it so you don't have to move."

This was apparently the right thing to say, for the two children sprang from their perch on the steps as if their bottoms were scalded and rushed into the house crying out for Mam and anyone else that would listen.

"Why did you say that?" Ethan said, voice hard. "You know we can't promise any such thing."

Emily shrugged. "I didn't promise. I just said we might. And that's why we're doing this, right? To see if we can stop it from happening?"

A large woman with a halo of hair sauntered out from inside, wiping her hands on a towel.

"What do you want?" she said, but her tone was more amused than unfriendly. The two children peered around her backside, their white teeth flashing.

"My name's Emily Tuttle and this is my brother Ethan. We're working for Ben Tuttle, who is a broadcaster looking into the demolition of this end of Geertsen Street. He thinks there may be something funny going on, and we are asking around to see if we can get the story from the people who actually live here." She took a step backward down the stoop, so she and Ethan stood on the same level.

The woman towered over them, and her eyes said she didn't entirely trust them. "Something is more than funny, if you ask me. None of us here," she said, waving her hand at the building behind her, "think there's anything funny at all about losing our house."

"No ma'am," Emily said. "I can understand that. We just want to find out all we can so that if there's a way to stop it, we can find it."

"Stop it?" the woman laughed loud enough that it echoed off the building across the street. "You can't stop it. You can chain yourself to that lamppost there if you want, but those bulldozers will come all the same. We've tried everything and nothing works. They want their shiny ballparks, and there's nothing we can do about it."

Emily shifted as if she was turning to go. Ethan stepped up one stair and said, "How long have they been telling you you had to leave?"

The woman rolled her eyes upward, thinking. "Six months? It was winter, that's all I can really remember. There's a paper, though, someplace." She made no move to get it.

Emily said, "I'd love to see that paper. Maybe if we could get the timeline down, we could figure out what their plan was."

The woman cracked her neck. "No point to that. It's easy enough to see what they want, and they're going to get it. It was like this in Detroit, too, where we came from. The powerful people on the City Council get it in their mind to have something, and they go and get it. We don't matter, us little people here on the edges."

Emily tried one more time. "I know it seems like that, but really, our uncle is a popular broadcaster. People listen to him. Powerful people. If you could just help us a little, we might be able to help you."

"She said my braids was pretty," Shiana said, from back by the doorway.

"Are pretty," the mother said, but her tone softened. "Well, it can't do any good, but you can come on in and I'll find that paper. I'm Mrs. Douglass, by the way."

She then turned and disappeared back into the apartment. Shiana and her brother held the door open, faces cracked wide with smiling. "Mam likes you," Shiana said, mostly to Emily. "I like you, too."

Emily bent as she passed and whispered, "It's because we're magical spirits, you and me. We use our powers to help people be happy. I can tell you're very good at it."

Shiana looked skeptical. "Magic spirits?"

Emily cocked an eyebrow. "You bet. I always know a magical spirit when I see one."

Shiana's face went from skeptical to wonderstruck, and she dashed ahead to the door of the apartment, flinging it wide.

"You're really something, you know that?" Ethan said sourly.

"Thank you," Emily said. "Magical spirits defy convention. We show up in the most unexpected places."

"I'll say."

"Shhhh."

The apartment was spare, without a lot of furniture, but it was neat as a pin and decorated with flair and original artwork. One whole wall of the family room was covered in a riot of colors and shapes, from cut snowflakes to poster-sized cutouts in every shade of the rainbow.

"Wow," Ethan said. "That magical spirit thing is real."

"Of course it is," Emily said. "Did you both do these?" The children nodded their heads so hard she thought they might fall off. For five minutes, they proceeded to tell the Tuttles everything about every scrap of paper on the wall. Where they made it. What it was. Where they got the paints, or crayons, or markers.

Mam came back in the middle of the performance. "Now, you two, let the guests have a minute to breathe," she said, but her voice was soft and full of pride.

"Your children are amazing," Ethan said, earning a smile from Shiana.

"Thank you, young man. I like to think so." She waved a paper in their direction. "I found it. Took some rummaging, but I found it. December 17, like I said. Back in the winter."

"May I?" Emily said.

"Knock yourself out. Won't do you any good, but you're welcome to see if it jogs anything loose."

The letter was printed on standard white paper, with the city letterhead at the top. "Dear Resident," it started.

"Very personal," Emily said dryly.

The letter said that the city had declared the entire end of the block, from the middle of the street down to the waterfront, as blighted, and had acquired the properties from the landlord. They were proceeding to eliminate the existing buildings, and the residents had until the first of June to vacate. Sincerely.

Emily looked up at the mother. "This is all they sent?"

"That's it. We got a yellow sticky notice on the front door a couple of weeks ago. That didn't last long, I can tell you. And no, I don't have it."

Ethan drew his camera out of his bag and took a photo of the letter. He handed it back. "It looks legal," he said.

"I'm sure it is," the mother said, sighing. "But legal doesn't keep my kids in the neighborhood. I know what they're doing. It's the new ballparks, isn't it?"

"Yes," Emily said.

"I know they think it will make things better down here, but it won't. I know this part of town. They can put gleaming new buildings here and dress them up in neon and flags, but people down here—and most of us will stay here, someplace—we don't care about that.

What we need is jobs and schools, not baseball. No
offense, if you're baseball players."

"She is," Ethan said.

"No offense taken," Emily said. "It's kind of baseball
that brought us here."

"When you'd rather be out at the pool or some
such, I shouldn't wonder. Still, here you are. You need to
understand, because my guess is you don't come from
this part of town, that the economics don't support
this ballpark idea at all. It will look pretty, but it will sit
empty most of the time."

"Neighborhood kids can play on it, at least," Emily
said, but the mother shook her head.

"Not kids from this neighborhood. They'll never see
the inside of that ballpark except when they're giving
tickets away. Yes, kids will play on it, some, but those
kids will come from the other side of town, where you're
probably from."

"Actually," Ethan said, "We're from Spoonerville."

The mother laughed. "Well, this is an experience
then. Trust me, that field won't be used more than
a dozen times all year. They already have a stadium
for the minor league team, and they won't be coming
down here."

"I think they plan to," Emily said.

"Won't matter if they do."

"But… that would mean fifty or so games a season, right down here. Hundreds of thousands of fans. That has to do some good in the local community."

The mother shook her head. "First off, there's all this property they're going to demolish. That's millions of dollars wasted. Then the stadium itself, which will be some more millions. It will take a lot of ticket sales to make up that money."

"But jobs… There will be jobs from it, won't there?"

"While they build, sure—but there are no workers from here for those kinds of jobs. And once the stadium is built, what kinds of jobs will there be then? Playing baseball? No, those jobs are all taken. Team jobs, like PR or logistics? They already have people in those jobs, too. But we'll be expected to take jobs sweeping up the stands or selling peanuts or tickets or some such. The kinds of jobs we're always supposed to do."

"Then we'll just have to stop them from knocking down the buildings," Emily said. "You shouldn't lose your home so they can have a shiny new ballpark."

"But we will. Nothing we can do about it now."

"Maybe we can," Ethan said.

"What's that mean?"

"Well, look here. This letter says you have to move out by June 1. It's June 27. You're still here. Why?"

The mother rubbed her chin. "Like I said, they put the yellow notice on the door a couple weeks ago. I thought that would be it, but since then, they've left us alone."

"Something about that tells me there's more to this story," Ethan said. "We just have to find out what it is."

If you think they should find Uncle Ben, turn to page 79.

If you think they should interview others, turn to page 265.

Emily paced. In the back of her mind, she could hear Uncle Ben, and the worry in his voice about finding something he could use for his YouTube broadcast. What could she bring him? How could she show that she was worth the money he was paying?

She went back to the desk and tried to concentrate on the book the reference librarian had given her. The letters and numbers swam before her eyes. It was no use. Her legs jiggled and seemed to want to walk away without her. Sighing, she bowed to the inevitable and got up from her stack of books.

She took her notebook and a pencil and stalked off into the stacks.

First there was the unfairness of it all. She shouldn't be here. She shouldn't have to be here. All she did was belt a ball farther than anyone had ever hit one in that place. Shouldn't that have been a good thing? No one seemed to see it that way, but she felt aggrieved in the bottom of her soul.

Then there was this job. Uncle Ben was a good researcher and a very smart guy. He'd been working on this story for months and still wasn't sure he'd come up with anything. How could she possibly—even with Ethan working away in the other room—come up with something so quickly? She'd never be able to find something if Ben couldn't. Hadn't he been over all this material himself? She was sure he had.

Maybe it was a mistake coming to the library. Maybe she should have asked to go down to the waterfront and interview people there. Surely that would be more productive than this.

She was deep into the nonfiction section, back against the far wall. An iron stairwell led down to the lower floor. The wall was pockmarked by small windows, barely the size of her head, and through them she saw trees and grass and blue sky. The beauty of summer, and she was inside, missing it.

It made her blood boil.

She turned and, without thinking about it, kicked the metal bookshelf behind her. A metallic clang rang through the library, and she half-expected the librarians to come storming down upon her and drag her off in chains. But nothing happened. She put her head in her hands and started back to her books. Maybe she'd put them away and just tell Uncle Ben she couldn't do it. Maybe he wouldn't fire her.

To her right, something thunked down onto the lowest shelf.

She cocked her head and saw a small booklet, not a lot larger than her own notebook and about the same thickness, had wedged itself between the bottom shelf and the stack of books behind it. She crouched and reached back for it, pried it loose, and drew it out. With a start, she realized she was in exactly the same place she'd gotten the books about Malantown history. This booklet must have gotten stuck between some of the others.

On its faded yellow cover, the booklet read
Malantown Official Budget Figures and the dates that
matched the first ten years of the city's existence.

Curious, she flipped it open. It smelled of must and
old paper, a smell she knew from aged books in small
bookstores. One of her favorites. She smiled like one
does when greeting an old friend. She riffled through it.

It contained less than fifty pages, but they were
densely crammed with figures, and someone had
written in the margins in pencil, making commentaries.
She pursed her lips. That was a no-no in a library book,
she'd always been told. One page had a circle around
some figures for "Advertising and Public Relations" and
a line out to the margin with a question mark. Emily ran
her finger over the page. It was rough, as if it had been
very old, though the publication date couldn't have been
more than a few years ago.

She flipped to the back. More scribbling. More
cryptic notes. The last date for which there were numbers was almost twenty years ago.

Examining the booklet in detail told her nothing
more. There were no identifying marks on it, as if it had
been intended for an audience that would already know
where it came from. The library hadn't stamped it—every other book in the place had "Malantown Central"
on it someplace. This one was clean. Or, not exactly
clean—she knocked dust from the back cover and wiped
her hands on her jeans.

There wasn't anything about the booklet that said it was important, or even interesting. Just a book of budget figures, crammed onto a shelf of other historical material. But for a second it seemed that her hands tingled just a little holding the thing. It was obscure. Different. It hadn't been part of the regular collection. The librarian hadn't plucked it off the shelf and handed it to her, despite the fact that it was precisely the sort of thing she'd been asking for. Maybe he didn't know it was there. Maybe—she thought, with that thrill that comes from possibly finding that you're in the middle of a story just like the ones in your favorite books—maybe no one knew it was there. Maybe someone had stashed it, hoping that one day it would be found and a terrific scandal would be uncovered.

Nah. It was just a booklet. But it was something she hadn't had before, and it could add to her information and show that she'd been thorough. Anything more was just summer daydreaming. After all, she had the book with the official figures in it already. What difference could this one make?

She stood up, the pleasant, dull hum of the library around her, and walked back to her table, with its pile of boring books. She put the booklet under her notebook and drew the thick, official Malantown budget book in front of her, with its crisp, unsullied white pages. Turning to the first year's budget figures, she ran her finger down them and wrote the bottom-line numbers for receipts and expenditures in her notebook.

The little booklet had those numbers on page two. The itemization was much more detailed in the yellowing book, but the figures tallied. She wrote those to the side of the first set and went to year two.

But this time the figures were different.

She wondered if she'd made a mistake. After all, the official book did not have a tally of net receipts, just a column of tax receipts on one side and a marginally lower column of expenditures on the other. Emily pulled out her phone and tapped the numbers in to get a final figure and wrote it down.

It didn't matter. The little yellow booklet's numbers—which did have a final tally—weren't just a little different. They were very different, several tens of thousands of dollars different. How could that be?

She went to year three. The official book continued to show solid upward growth with no debt, precisely as a well-run city would. The yellow booklet, on the other hand, showed significant borrowing, running deficits of hundreds of thousands. Where the figures diverged the most, there would be a pencil mark and a comment in the margin: "altered," or "redacted," or "intent miscal." Some of the comments she couldn't read.

Emily sat and stared into the distance, over toward the brightly-colored children's area. What was this? And how could she get this information to Uncle Ben? Maybe he could make something out of it.

All of a sudden she felt nervous about having this booklet out on the table where people could see it, where the librarian could see it.

She stuffed it into her notebook, where it all but disappeared. Then she walked through the fiction section, turned right, and went into the ladies' bathroom.

She took a stall, locked the door, put the booklet on the (thankfully dry) floor, and pulled out her phone. Page by page, she photographed the entire thing.

"We've got some of these figures online," Uncle Ben said. "Just big categories, nothing fine like this book has." He pinched Emily's photo open wider. "But there's more, too. Look at these figures, here," he pointed. "You see this? These are different than the official figures." He looked up at her.

She nodded, a light in her eyes. "I saw that," she said. "But I don't know what it means."

Ethan held his own phone up, looking at the same things. "There's a Council purge ten years in. I read the official record—mass resignation is the story—but it seemed a little convenient. Only one guy remained. The other six quit, even the ones who had a couple years left on their terms. They didn't stick around, either. I checked on the Internet. None of them live in Malantown any more."

"That was twenty years ago," Emily said. "Hardly surprising."

"That's when this booklet runs out, it looks like," Uncle Ben said. He set the phone down on the desk and sat in his chair, rubbing his chin. "The most difficult part of this is that I don't know what the booklet means, really."

Emily made a face. He waggled a finger at her. "No, really. Listen. The official figures are what they are. There's no changing them, and there's no way to use this booklet to refute them. Not that I won't bring it up and see what kinds of monsters rise to the bait. But it's a long way from definitive proof that the Malantown government is corrupt."

"Proof enough for me," Ethan said.

Uncle Ben laughed. "Yeah, but you didn't need any convincing. The people of this town are a different story entirely. It will take more than this to do the job."

"Besides which," Emily said, "it still leaves a mystery. The government might have some people in it that are fudging the numbers to make themselves look good. But money is money. If it isn't in the bank, people start to notice. Since we believe it isn't in the bank, where is it?"

Uncle Ben put his feet on the desk and rocked back in his chair. "I don't know. There has to be another revenue source somewhere. If they'd raised taxes to handle it, people would have screamed bloody murder. It can't be that."

"Donations?" Emily said. "Maybe someone is bank-rolling the city."

"No," Uncle Ben said, "People take money out of government when they're corrupt. No one puts money in, at least not secretly. If you do something like that, you take a lot of credit. There would be publicity."

The three of them sat and thought, but for a long time there was only the hum of the air conditioning.

"What about bond issues?" Ethan said.

Uncle Ben turned an eye on him. "What bond issue?"

"About ten years back. There was some kind of bond thing the city proposed. It was supposed to be for schools and to pay off old debt by raising more taxes for the bond. It was in all the papers. It passed with a big majority."

"I remember that. Several tens of millions, if I recall. People talked about how many new schools that would build and how much they could upgrade the old ones."

"Well," Ethan said, warming up, "Suppose those schools didn't get built. Suppose the city spent the money retiring old bonds instead."

"Go on."

"There's no way to know," Ethan said, glancing over at Emily, "But I bet the city funded itself in the first twenty years not with tax revenue, but with bonds. I bet the city sold bonds, took the money, and used it to cover the budget shortfall. Then about ten years ago, those bonds came due. They didn't have the money to pay them, so they refinanced them with new bonds and used the school project as cover."

Uncle Ben dropped his feet to the floor and sat up. "That might work," he said. "But it's a shell game. If they do that, then the next round of bonds just moves the debt load farther down the timeline." He began pacing back and forth between the overstuffed filing cabinet and the whiteboard.

"It makes it bigger, too, doesn't it?" Emily said. She fidgeted, too. Adrenaline was making it hard to sit still.

Uncle Ben nodded, scratching his cheek. "Interest works that way."

Ethan took the opportunity to shift over to Uncle Ben's softer chair and leaned back in it. "I'm not sure I get how that happens. A bond... has to be repaid on a certain date, right?"

"Right." Uncle Ben went to the whiteboard and began to draw. "If a company or a government sells a bond, say, for $1000 at 5% with a 10-year maturity, it has to pay back that $1000 in ten years at 5% compounded interest, which is going to be something like $600. It can finance the government that way, but tax receipts have to grow by at least as much as the interest on the bond or the government is bleeding money."

"Then what is this 'debt retirement' thing?" Emily said.

"Simple. You use a new bond to pay off an old one. You sell more bonds and use the money to pay off the ones that are reaching maturity."

Emily's jaw dropped. "You can do that?"

Ethan laughed. "You can, but you really shouldn't."

"If you do, you're piling debt on debt. Just paying off the interest takes up an increasing share of the budget… Holy wow," Uncle Ben said. He gently capped the marker and laid it on the tray. He turned around, eyes shining. "That's what this is all about. The city needs the new stadiums to be approved so they can get a new round of bonds issued. Without something like that, they can't get enough subscription for a new bond. People won't buy them. They don't have the money to pay them back."

"The city is bankrupt," Ethan said, his voice soft and full of wonder.

"The city is bankrupt," Uncle Ben said. "They can't pay their bonds."

Uncle Ben didn't think his YouTube video would do enough to get the issue its appropriate level of press, so he called a couple of friends in the newspaper and a reliable city employee in the finance department. The presentation took place in his office, and it blew the doors off the building.

The twins had spent the previous two weeks collecting more data, looking for good sites to put in the video, and editing. It shocked Emily how many hours of editing went into every minute of video.

"I thought being a YouTube star sounded like fun," she said one late night as she stared bleary-eyed at the computer screen. "I think I'd rather haul garbage."

But the finished product, she had to admit, was worth it. The footage unrolled, with Uncle Ben on voiceover, explaining what they'd found, and interviewing a couple of Malantowners whose bonds were, indeed, expiring that year. "They've told us there's nothing to worry about," one woman said, in a voice that said clearly that she didn't believe the city.

"In the end, whether the city is putting on this bid process to attract big investors to build new ballfields, or for some other purpose, the city books should get a thorough examination." And with that, the video was over.

The room was silent. The city employee sat, ashen-faced, and ran his hands through his hair. The newspaper men exchanged glances, their faces blossoming grins. One of them pulled his phone out and began tapping. The other said, "Who are these two?" pointing at the twins.

"Ethan Tuttle."

"Emily Tuttle."

"My crack researchers. It was Emily that found the smoking gun," Uncle Ben said. He turned to the city employee. "Well?" he said.

The man pursed his lips. "I know... well, I know a lot less than I think I should. You have to understand. This isn't easy for me to do. I don't even know what I can do, you know, with everyone at the city.... What will they think? How do I even start asking the right questions?" He looked about somewhat wildly, as if he no longer knew exactly where he was.

"I know this is hard, Don. I wouldn't have asked you here if I didn't know that you were the kind of person that cares more about the truth than about his own neck."

Don laughed ruefully. "I don't know that. How can you know that?"

"I'm very smart."

The meeting broke up, the men shaking hands and the newspapermen asking the Tuttles some questions, saying they'd be in touch.

When they were gone, the three of them sat in the office sipping cans of soda, their eyes alight. "What do you think will happen?" Emily said.

"I have no idea. But we put a lot of work in, and I think things are going to be very different," Uncle Ben said. "Whatever happens, you guys have been fantastic. Best assistants I've ever had."

"So," Ethan said, "This is a permanent gig, then? Because we need a job for a long time."

"It's yours as long as you want it," Uncle Ben said.

But things didn't go the way they hoped. There was some press, a couple of articles. One of the local TV stations picked up the story and did some interviews. The Mayor denied anything was wrong and said the budget was fine. The bid process was long and expensive, but the benefits to the town would be immense. Yes, they were likely to need to bond for the stadiums, but those bonds would pay off handsomely. Just think of the shops, the restaurants, the prestige!

And he was very convincing. So convincing that the Tuttles themselves shrugged and wanted to believe him. It all sounded so good.

"But it's not. It never is. We've done the research, remember. New ballparks look great and never make money. Never. Nowhere. Surely not in Malantown."

Don, down at the city, called a couple of weeks later. "I can't ask any more questions. Everything I've been able to get my hands on looks fine. I don't think there's anything funny going on." Uncle Ben thought he sounded sorry, but he wasn't going to get anywhere.

And then it was too late to do anything more, because the international bid committee was there, and Malantown rolled out the red carpet.

They got the bid. Just down the block, the bulldozers rolled. They spent the next two weeks boxing everything up. "Where are you going to move to?" Ethan said.

"There's a small office complex in downtown Spoonerville," Uncle Ben said. "The rent is exorbitant, but we can probably figure it out." He surveyed the empty office, ran his palm over a desk as if trying to summon a spirit. His face showed only disappointment.

"We did all we could," Emily said. "And hey, maybe it won't be a disaster. Maybe the tournament will be a success and the whole world will want to come to quaint little Malantown and spend millions of dollars."

"Maybe flying monkeys will descend on the city and carry everyone off to a forbidding castle where enslaved guards march around singing O-EE-O," Ethan said. His face stayed in the same despairing set it had been in since the news came in.

"More likely, all the heavy trucks bringing in equipment will collapse one of the rotting bridges and drop everyone into the river. So we have that to look forward to," Uncle Ben said. He laughed. "Please do not for a moment believe that I'm being serious."

Emily switched off a light. The rear storage room went dark. "I'm just sad that we're losing our jobs. I still have a lot of money to pay to the church."

Uncle Ben took a ring of keys from around his neck and dropped them on the desk inside the front door. He flicked off the last of the lights, and stepped through the door, holding it open for the twins. "You know, I've been thinking about that. It sure was handy to have you two around for research and legwork. I got more done the last few weeks than I have in years. Money's going to be tight, for sure. I don't know that I can pay you as much as I have, but would you still do projects for me? It might be as much as half what you have been getting. It's not much, but—"

"It's still something," Ethan said. "I'm in. Just think, Em! Now it will take twelve years to pay for your homer, instead of just six!"

Uncle Ben locked the door.

THE END

Foghorn's Chicken Shack was only too glad to see Emily come through the door. A harried woman, her hair back in a severe bun and grease stains all over her apron, took one look at her and said, "You're hired. Unless you're here for a bucket."

"No, no bucket," Emily said, glancing back at Mom. "I came because of a job."

"God be praised," the woman said, wiping her hands on a towel. She extended one of them. "Carla Popewell. I'm the manager."

"Emily Tuttle."

"You ever worked in a fast food joint before, Emily?"

Emily shook her head. Carla waved her hand, dismissing it. "Not important. What's sixteen times five?"

"Uh... Eighty?"

"Hallelujah," Carla said. "You can do that in your head, you can do anything in this place without the smallest trouble. I'll have you on the register in two weeks. Meanwhile, come with me back to the office, and let's get the blessed paperwork handled."

Emily had little choice but to follow the woman back through the steaming, oily kitchen to a small rear office with a sticker on the door that said, imaginatively, "Office."

Ten minutes later, Mrs. Tuttle left the Shack with a smile on her face and a promise to return at three in the afternoon to pick up her daughter.

Emily, for her part, got a hair net, an apron, and an order form for a t-shirt. "I don't really know how any of this works," she said, for the fifteenth time.

"You don't have to—I know. I tell you what to do, and you do it. It's a remarkably simple operation. After a month or so, you will know everything and you will start telling me. For now, sign that thing and let's get to work. Lunch rush is coming."

They exited the office and took up a position in the kitchen in front of a deep-fat fryer. Carla pointed to a huge rack stacked with plastic bags containing brown lumps. Cold radiated off them. It was at least ten degrees cooler next to that rack than anywhere else in the sweltering kitchen.

"Chicken," she said to the rack. "Fryer," she said, looking down at the vat. "Right here is the setting you want. You put the chicken in the metal basket, you hit the button that says start, then you put the basket in the fryer." She demonstrated. "In seven minutes, the fryer starts buzzing like a demented hornet. You take one of these gloves, put it on, and take the basket out. Dump the chicken here and do the whole thing again. If this is all you do today, you'll save my life."

Emily thought she could probably do that much.

It was far from glamorous, but it was eight dollars an hour. By eleven o'clock, Emily's hair was matted to her head, and her feet ached from standing in the same place. There hadn't even been a lot of customers, Emily

didn't think, and yet every piece of chicken she made had gone out the door somehow. People came in in twos and threes, but instead of buying a couple of pieces, they'd buy a whole bucket, sixteen pieces at a time. Twenty-two dollars.

Things got worse. Emily mastered running one vat, so Carla let her run the second vat as well, churning out chicken batches on a staggered three-and-a-half minute rotation for what seemed like days. Carla brought Emily a big drink at noon and let her eat a sandwich a half an hour later on a fifteen-minute break.

The traffic slowed after one, and by two hardly anyone was coming in any more. Carla turned the register over to Pete and the cooking over to Angela, and sat down in the dining area with Emily. She handed her an ice cream sundae, soft-serve drizzled in chocolate.

"You did very well today, Emily. We needed you and that's no lie."

Emily dipped her spoon into the sundae. "I didn't do that much."

"You made chicken by the barrel, and that's what we do here. This isn't Chez Louis. We pump out crispy-fried chicken in its super-salty coating, and people buy it because it's crave-worthy and filling. It's not art. But it's food. We were short-handed and you made a big difference."

"It doesn't seem worth it," Emily said. "I'm beat, and people came in and bought up that chicken in just a couple minutes. It took a lot longer for me to make it than it took them to buy it. That's not fair."

Carla slipped off her cap. "Labor theory of value. Very Marxist."

Emily stared. "What?"

"Look, kid, you seem like a smart cookie. You've obviously learned some stuff kicking around, and you talk like you come from an educated house. I know I don't look like much, but I've been to school. There are two major theories about how prices should work." Carla put the salt and pepper like poles of a battery in the middle of the table. "This here is Marx," pointing to the pepper, "and his theory is that a thing ought to cost what it takes to make it. Like, um—"

"A stained-glass window."

Carla narrowed her eyes. "Okay, that's pretty random, but let's say a stained-glass window. It costs, I dunno, about ten grand to make. Just to choose a number. That pays for the time of the craftsman, the materials, stuff like that. Marx says we should price that thing at the cost to make it."

"Sounds good. I mean, I guess Marx couldn't have been wrong about everything."

"You think?" Carla shrugged. "That's your look-out. Anyway, over here we have the market theory of value. This one comes from Ludwig von Mises and some others." She pointed to the salt. "It says that the price of a thing ought to be whatever the seller and the buyer agree on. Since you brought up the stained glass window thing, let's say it's one of those really old ones, made by Michelangelo."

"He didn't make stained glass."

Carla's eye twitched a couple times. "Whatever. Leonardo, then. Don't tell me, he didn't make stained glass, either. You get the point. The church that owns that window, they've got a piece of history. It means something to them more than glass and lead and labor. You know what I mean. It's special. So they might charge $100,000 for that window."

"A hundred grand?" Emily sneered. "No way is anyone going to pay that."

"Maybe not. But if they don't, then no sale. The church is okay with that. And along comes a fellow who has a lifelong dream to own a piece of history,

LUDWIG VON MISES

KARL MARX

something that Leonardo's hands have touched. So he's willing to pay, and he buys the window."

"He's an idiot."

"One man's idiot is another man's cockeyed fool. Anyway, that's the theory. Now which one actually works in the real world?"

"Marx does, sorry to say."

"Does he? Let's try that out with some chicken. You made a bucket's worth. How much do we charge for it?"

"$22."

"And how much does it cost us to make. Your time, by the way, is about seventy-five cents for the 7 minutes of frying."

"The chicken costs something."

"But not much. It's about .90 a pound, and a bucket is two pounds of chicken."

"The bucket isn't free."

"That's a nickel. Seriously."

Emily furrowed her brow a second. "So that's right around $3, a little less."

Carla nodded. "We make about $19 a bucket. Now, it's not all gravy. We have to pay for this place," she said, waving an arm, "and some of my time for supervising you, but all told, that bucket doesn't cost us more than $6. Sixteen dollars of profit. Should we lower our prices?"

Emily marked time by eating some more sundae. "That's up to you."

"If we ask Mr. Marx here, what's he going to say?"

"Definitely. You're making an obscene profit."

"We're making an obscene profit. You work for the man now. What would the salt say?"

"People want to pay. We want to sell. The price is where those two things meet. So it's okay."

"You got it. My question is, which of these two condiments are you?"

Emily twirled the pepper, thinking. "I don't know. I guess there's a good reason to sell our chicken at that price. But it seems like there are hungry people who don't buy it because it's too expensive. And if our chicken were cooked by Michelangelo..." She shot a glance at Carla, who laughed out loud. "Then we might charge $50 a bucket or something, and that wouldn't be fair at all."

"Why not?"

"Because... because we're making so much money! It's way more than it costs to make it. We could lower our price and be more fair."

"That guy," Carla said, pointing over to the corner where a bald man sat eating a sandwich, "seems very pleased with the deal. Should we not do business?"

"Wouldn't he be more pleased if it were cheaper?"

"Maybe. But I wouldn't be. This price is where both sides meet on the happy meter. We're both perfectly content to do business at this price. Why shouldn't we?"

"Because what if the guy doesn't have the money?" Emily could hear her voice getting shrill, but she couldn't stop it. "Then there's no deal."

"Right. Then we should lower our price for that guy."

"What? That's not fair at all."

Carla laughed again, big and throaty, like she did everything. "You can't have it both ways. Either we should do business where everyone is happy, or we shouldn't. If we go with Marx, we set a static price for what it cost to make the thing. But I don't want to sell at that price. It doesn't compensate me for the risk of running this place. It doesn't give me enough profit to handle disasters and emergencies. And frankly, although my wage is X, what I want as compensation for all this hassle is much more than X, and if I don't get it, I won't open the restaurant. Then nobody gets anything. Is that fair?"

"It's more fair than changing your price every time someone comes in the door."

Carla wiped her hands and cleaned the table with a rag from her apron. "Then we have different definitions of fair. I get the feeling this is kind of personal to you."

"What? No, I don't... It doesn't matter," Emily said.

"Whatever you say. All I can tell you is that if I had a stained-glass window made by Leonardo, and you tried to buy it for $10,000, you'd have to pry it from my cold, dead fingers. Things are more than just what you can replace them with. You have things like that, whether you know it or not. They have value above leather or wood or tin. That value matters in the market. If it didn't, you wouldn't have a job." She pushed back from the table. "And right now, you need to get back to it. You owe me an hour, yet."

Emily put in that hour by cleaning things. Thick yellow latex gloves kept the harsh chemicals off, but the ammonia stung her eyes and made her nose run. When Mom came to pick her up, she was a mess.

"You look like a torture victim. Was it that bad?" Mom said, her arms folded across her chest.

"Worse," Emily said, taking Mom's hand and leading her back to the small locker room where she changed out of her greasy work clothes.

"At least you made some money."

"Not enough to matter."

Mom laughed. "Matter to what? You have something you desperately need to pay for in the next couple weeks?"

Emily hung her apron on a peg and shut her locker. There was no point in locking it; everything in it belonged to the store. "It's not that," she said, leaning against the cool of the gray metal. "It's just a lot of work for not very much money, is all."

"You wouldn't have made a dime at home. Nor accomplished anything, neither."

"What did I accomplish here, besides filling orders all day?"

"Five hours of the day, which is technically only about 20% of it. And people have food in their bellies, which they wouldn't have if you hadn't been here to provide it."

"They'd have managed. Or they could have gone to MacBurger or something."

"Where, no doubt, a young girl is standing in the locker room complaining that her work has been unrewarded." Mom rubbed Emily's shoulders a second. "I'm proud of you, though, so that makes it all worth it."

Emily tried to laugh at that, but all that came out was a kind of snorty chuckle.

The locker room door opened, and Carla stood framed in the doorway. "Oh. Mrs. Tuttle. I'm glad you're here. Your daughter is a jewel beyond price, and you may quote me."

"Thanks for noticing. I thought I was the only one who could see it," Mom said.

"You'd have seen it if you'd watched her cranking out the batches of chicken earlier today. We had one devil of a lunch rush, and without Emily here we'd have been in the soup."

Mom patted Emily's back. Emily pulled herself away from the blessed cool of the locker and tried to smile.

"She's on the schedule the rest of the week, right through lunch, if she can be here. State law won't let me work her more than 30 hours, but I can promise her that many pretty much every week, if she wants it."

Mom said, "Oh, she does. Thank you very much." She gave Emily's arm a squeeze.

As soon as they got in the car, Emily said, "I don't want to go back."

"Unsurprising," Mom said as she buckled her seat belt. "And yet you will."

"Why?" Emily wailed. "What is all this for? Is this so you can get some kind of evil parent medal?"

"The secret is out, apparently. I'll have to alert evil parent security to come pick you up."

Emily unbuckled her seatbelt and reached for the car door handle. Mom put the car in gear and backed out of the parking lot. Emily's look would have frozen Arundel, but she clipped her seatbelt back where it belonged. Mom's face registered nothing.

They traveled down the road for a few minutes before Mom finally said, "Okay, Em. The truth is that I don't want to make you do something you're going to hate. But you're not yourself. Is something wrong?"

"No."

Mom glanced over at Emily, sitting like a block of wood in the passenger seat. "See, this is precisely why I ask. This isn't like you, sweetheart. Are you sure there's nothing wrong? Did Ethan do something to you, and you've got this silly notion that you're going to get him back yourself instead of getting your parents involved?"

"No, Ethan hasn't done anything. It's not anything anyone did. I'm just sick of summer, and I don't want to do anything but sit in my room and read. I'm not hormonal and I'm not going through a phase or whatever else your books tell you is probably wrong with me. I'm fine. Everything's fine."

"Clearly."

"Fine. Don't believe me."

The trees and houses rolled past the window. Emily saw none of them. All she could see was chicken going into a vat of oil. Every so often, the surface of the vat looked like the window of Our Lady church.

She could tell Mom. Mom would understand.

And then Mom would make her pay a hundred thousand dollars—or worse, she and Dad would do it themselves—or whatever the sum was that the church wanted for their stupid window. She'd be working at the Chicken Shack for the rest of her life. She couldn't face it.

But wouldn't it be better than this? She ached and there was a continuous burning in her gut. Nothing tasted good. She looked out at the bright summer sunshine and thought about baseball and the pool and all the things she'd looked forward to doing. None of them appealed to her. She wanted nothing more than to just curl up in a ball.

It would go away. Of course it would. The church would get their window, and everything would go back to normal, plus she wouldn't have to work for the rest of her life paying off something that wasn't her fault. It might take a long time, but eventually it would be fine.

Or she could tell Mom now, when the freakout wouldn't matter much because she was already miserable.

Emily bit her lip.

If you think she should tell Mom, turn to page 209.

If you think she shouldn't, turn to page 11.

Church was often boring. That was the main thing. They sat there on their uncomfortable pews and a man—it was usually a man—would spout off some stuff about God that had been said a dozen times in the recent past. And people would listen along, then sing and go home, and what did it all mean, anyway?

Emily stared at the wall next to her bed and tried to think what she should do. There wasn't any reason to go to church, was there? Other than that her family just always went. They all did. They always had. What would it mean if she didn't go?

And, anyway, she was really tired. And her throat was scratchy. That probably meant she was starting to get a cold. If she was, then she might not be able to go to work tomorrow, and she was scheduled for a full shift. She didn't know anyone's phone numbers—except Marcus's, and she knew he was already scheduled to work—so she couldn't get anyone to cover for her, and that would mean that she would end up just skating on it, and Carla would be mad and fire her. Then she'd have no job. Jesus didn't want her to have no job, did He?

She thought of Jesus with the capitals, every time—like some foreign royalty she didn't know, rather than someone familar. It was just how it was. And truthfully—if she'd been interested in the truth at all at the moment—there was a part of her that knew He deserved those capital letters, and the respect they signaled.

But Jesus didn't want her to lose her job, right? Perhaps she'd better sleep. In her bed, that was, not in church. It was hard to sleep there, anyway, because where did you put your head? On the pew in front? What if the horrid Pertwee boy colored your hair orange while you were sleeping? What if you woke up with a mashed-pink line across your forehead? What if you snored?

No. If she was going to sleep—the more she thought of it, the more she was sure she needed to—she should do it at home. Was that a cough? Yes, she was going to cough, for sure. The more she concentrated on her throat, the more she needed to. It busted out of her all at once, bursting the dam.

Mom walked in. Perfect timing.

"You coming?" Mom was in her Sunday best, a sharp-creased skirt below a floral blouse, her hair swept back and bangs straightened. She looked marvelous. She always did on Sundays.

But Emily was annoyed at the question, simple as it was. Hadn't she heard the cough? Wasn't she worried about Emily's health? "I'm sick," Emily said. "My throat hurts and I'm coughing."

"Pollen will do that," Mom said. "Pollen and attitude. Shockingly powerful, those things. Well, if you change your mind, I'll be back between meetings to check on you. I'd like it if you'd come. You'll miss your friends and they'll miss you."

"I'm just not feeling well. I'll go next time."

Mom came over, as Emily had known she would, and put a cool hand on Emily's forehead. "No fever," she said. It didn't sound like she'd thought there would be one. "That's good, anyway. I'll tell God you said hello."

Emily chuckled, then remembered that should hurt and turned it into a kind of strangled throat-clearing.

Mom left. Emily heard the footsteps down the stairs, and the front door closing. There was something final in it.

She hadn't actually meant to sleep, come to that, but there was Mom, closing the door and going out again. Had Mom actually come in? Was she dreaming? She sat up fast and ran a hand over her face. The bedside clock said 10:30. She'd been asleep for almost an hour.

See? She really was tired and needed the sleep. Her head was stuffed with cotton and her mouth felt like something furry had died there.

But if she got up before Mom left again, Mom would try to talk her into going back for Sunday School, and that she was not going to do. Why did Mom care, anyway? Was it that big a deal?

Marcus wasn't there on Monday. That left the Shack short staffed, and everyone was cranky. Topping it off, there had been twice the usual rush, so everyone stood in their spots for hours and breaks were hard to come by.

Carla apologized and sent Fred across the street to get everyone shakes after the lunch rush finally died down.

"I know we make them here, but let's face it, The Shakedown is better," she said.

"You did great today," Carla said as Emily left. Carla's face was pink, her hair matted. She looked like she'd run a marathon.

Emily smiled but she was too tired to care. She got out of there as fast as she could, and tried not to think about having to go back the next day.

Marcus called her two days later. "Sorry about ducking out on you guys like that," he said, not sounding at all like he really was, "but my cousin's neighbor called me Sunday and offered me this sweet job that pays way more than the stinkin' shack. I think I can get you in, too, if you want it."

"What kind of work is it?" she said.

"It's a window and siding place. They need people to go around and schedule appointments to come out and do estimates for new windows. That's our part. Easy. We don't even have to do any selling. We just walk around and talk to people."

Outside. In the sun. Emily almost begged. "That sounds incredible."

"Can you come down here to the shop tomorrow?"

Emily said she could and wrote down the address.

"It will be nice to see you," Marcus said. "We'll get you out of the steaming fry hole."

Emily blushed, grateful that Marcus couldn't see her. "I'd like that," she said. "And, you know, to see you again. It's boring at the shack without you."

She went downstairs to find Mom. "I have a job interview tomorrow," she said. "Can you take me? I could ride my bike, I guess. I don't think it's too far."

"That would be nice," Mom said. "Tomorrow's a busy day for me."

Emily checked the GPS and the electronic map told her that biking would take her fifteen minutes. But then she wondered how it would look to Marcus to have her ride up on her pink five-speed. What was nearby? There was a bus stop half a block away. If there was a bike rack, she could put her bike there and walk the rest of the way.

She walked in the next day right on time, and there was Marcus, sitting on the edge of a desk, with a man in a checked shirt and an artful scruff on his face sitting behind it.

"Told you," Marcus said. "She's a square."

"If that means on time for things," the man said, standing, "that would be a nice change." He extended his hand. "Frank Millner."

"Emily Tuttle."

"I've heard a lot about you, Emily. Have a seat." He smiled and gestured to a faux-leather chair in front of the desk. "I assume Marcus here has told you about the job?"

Emily nodded. "It sounds great."

"There are some quirks. I don't have a lot of work here at the moment," Millner said. "Most people don't replace their windows unless something happens, like they break a couple, or someone can explain why the new ones are actually going to save them money." He leaned back in his chair.

"People don't break enough windows, I guess, so we're going to have to explain the benefits to them. If I can't drum up some more work, things could get hairy. So I'm willing to invest a little bit in you two to see if you can drum up some business for us." He told her about the programs and the windows they offered. "You'll work this part of town, one of you on one side of the street, and the other on the other. The pay is $15 an hour, with bonuses depending on how successful you are. You'll work twenty hours a week, at least eight of those on the weekends."

"Saturday, you mean?" Emily clarified.

"Saturday and Sunday. Sunday morning is the best time of the week to catch people at home." He saw the look on Emily's face and said, "That's not a problem, is it?"

Emily hurriedly shook her head. "No, it's not a problem. I mean, my mother won't like it, but... uh, she can just deal with it. Because this is business, right?"

Millner paused, his eyes on her. "Right," he finally said.

"A kid grows up. You can't put them in chains forever," Emily said, the saying of it making her bold.

"That's it," Marcus said, patting her shoulder. "I'll show you the ropes when you're ready. We're going to make a great team."

They did, too, at least in sales. Emily watched as the business began to flourish. At first, Mom was adamant that Emily was not going to work on Sunday, but she came around. Emily went the first few weeks to an earlier church meeting, but after a while, she stopped that, too. She'd work her side of the street, racking up leads for the company, then she and Marcus would have lunch together. She rode home in his car, his hand close to hers on the seat. She imagined she could feel the heat of it, like it was electric.

Then Marcus had an idea.

"You know, we'd have a lot more business if some of these people understood how much better off they'd be with our windows. But their windows are just fine, so they think they don't need us."

"What are you going to do? Go back and try to convince them?"

Marcus smirked. "Not exactly."

"What, then?"

He laughed. "You wouldn't like it. You're too much of a square. But trust me, it's going to be big."

Three days later, Millner called them both to his desk. "I've got a new set of routes for you. We're going to go back to the place we started and go through it again."

Emily raised her eyebrows. "Again? Won't those people be angry that we're bugging them?"

"I don't think so," Millner said, a gleam in his eye. "Things have changed a bit." He pointed at the local paper, featuring an article that showed a broken window and a sad homeowner. Emily picked it up.

Several homes in the area had had their windows broken in the last couple days. Not the same window every time, either, but an apparently random selection, broken in different ways, some with a bb gun, some

FRIDAY, SEPT 2 - DAILY EDITION - $250
SPOONERVILLE'S ANNUAL GOLF FUND RAISER BRINGS WATER TO AFRICA

The City Herald
Spoonerville's trusted news source since 1913

Malantown wins IBA contract
Waterfront to be revived with the construction of new stadiums / parking

SIDNEY BURNS
CITY RELATIONS

Window Vandals At Large
Police are pursuing a number of leads and expect to make an arrest at any moment

with rocks, and one with a small dog. Police were still trying to figure that one out. The paper read, "police are pursuing a number of leads and expect to make an arrest at any moment."

Emily looked up. She knew that verbiage. The paper had said the same thing when the Our Lady window was broken. It was code for "nobody knows anything, and there isn't any way to find out who did it."

"Right. So it appears that these people need windows now, and I propose that we take advantage of that to get them some."

Marcus took the paper and read. "Good thing this happened. Broken windows are a good thing for the economy."

Emily shook her head. "It's not good for those people. Now they're out the cost of the window."

"But we get the business," Millner said. "That means we can pay you guys, and the guys in back. The money isn't gone. It still spreads through the economy and helps all kinds of people."

Emily knew there was something wrong with this idea. "No, but that's the wrong way to think about it. I mean, if broken windows were really good for the economy, then why don't we have gangs run around and break windows all the time. For that matter, why not have them crash cars and light homes on fire, too?"

Millner coughed. "Gangs that go around breaking windows? Sounds like we *do* have that."

Emily shot a glance at Marcus. He studied the paper and wouldn't meet her eyes, but she thought she detected a smug look before he smothered it with newsprint.

"And what harm is it doing? Actually, I think it's doing good for a lot of people," Marcus said from behind the paper.

"Again, except the homeowners."

"But they were just going to blow that money on something else. Maybe on a bucket of chicken," Marcus said.

Emily thought of the Chicken Shack with a strong sense of guilt. "But then Carla doesn't get that money."

"Someone else will go stuff their face with chicken instead. What's it to you?" Marcus said. "You'd rather those people give their cash to the Chicken Shack than to us?"

"You can't get out of it that way. If I'm Patty Homeowner, and I have a window and money, I can get chicken, too, and then I have a window and chicken. This way, I have to use the cash just to get back to where I was already. People have to spend money running in place. That's not progress. It's not making things better."

Millner grabbed the paper. "Whatever. I don't care about economics. And you're not making things better sitting here reading the news. Get out there and make us proud."

Riding out to the neighborhood in Marcus' car, Emily couldn't shake the feeling that he knew something about the broken windows.

And then she remembered that she knew something about another broken window.

So she couldn't ask.

The weather was perfect, sun pouring down. The homeowners were only too glad to have someone come and give them an estimate on the cost of new windows. "We sure need them," one fellow said. "Terrific timing, you coming along today."

"Terrific," Emily said.

It was her best day selling so far. Marcus', too. He crowed about it, and held Emily's hand while she sat next to him in the front of his car. A dark pit growled in her stomach and wouldn't go away.

Probably, she thought, it will never go away.

Millner was ecstatic and gave them both bonuses.

Marcus drove her home and kissed her on the cheek. "Nothing but sunshine and roses from here on out," he said, exultant. "You and me, Em. Together we can do anything."

Emily tried to smile, but her cheeks were made of lead. Mom greeted her with a hug and a "there's my hard-working girl. Dinner in ten minutes."

Emily went upstairs, curled up on her bed, and cried.

THE END

"I'm going over there," Emily said. She handed her cap and her bat to Ethan. "Take these home, and I'll see you later. Sometime. If they don't kill me and bury me under the church."

Ethan sighed and handed back the gear. "I'm not letting you face the music by yourself. I'll go with you and maybe the two of us together can think of some way to get you out of it, since you're going to be all noble."

They trudged up the side of the vacant lot toward the wounded church, walking their bikes and listening to the sirens approach. They reached the old stone building at just about the same time as the police car. A pair of uniformed policemen stepped out of the vehicle, their faces grim and purposeful. They saw the Tuttles walking up, bats in hand, and immediately their eyes narrowed.

The older one, grey hair sticking out from under his cap, said, pointing to the window, "You two know something about this?"

Emily swallowed loud enough for Ethan to hear it. "Yes," she said simply.

The policeman waited a moment, but she said nothing more. Since she had no idea what they would want to know, she felt like volunteering information was probably a bad idea. The officer's name tag said "Coleridge." He looked over toward the vacant lot, then back to the Tuttles.

He spoke to Ethan. "You hit the ball out here?" he said, as if he didn't really believe it.

"No," Ethan said. "She did."

"She's a lefty?" Coleridge said.

"She just has good power to the opposite field," Ethan said.

The cop appraised the distance again. "Apparently." Then he recovered himself. "But this, this is a serious thing. This window is older than the town. There's no telling how much it cost."

In this, though, he was wrong. There was telling. Father MacGillivray knew almost to the penny. "Sixteen thousand, four hundred seventeen dollars, give or take," he said, once the party was all gathered.

Mr. Tuttle raised his eyebrows. He and Mrs. Tuttle had hustled right down as soon as the twins had called them from the Father's office telephone. "That's a fairly precise number, Father. I'm surprised you know so exactly."

Father MacGillivray shrugged. "We had an appraisal done not very long ago, for insurance purposes. The insurers concluded there was no value they could assign to such a priceless artifact. But they did urge us to consult with a stained-glass manufactory to determine what it would cost to replace it, in the event that should become necessary. We ran several scenarios. This particular disaster isn't far from one of those we discussed."

Rain dripped through the rent in the window. The storm had come and gone, but the damage was still being done.

"Insurance will pay for the replacement, I take it," Mr. Tuttle said.

"They will. But we have a deductible of $5,000, and our rates will go up. We would prefer not to make a claim at all. In the end, this is the responsibility of the children. They broke the window."

"*She* broke the window," Ethan said, under his breath. "I was standing on second base."

Mother shushed him. "That's a lot of money for a fifteen-year old," she said to the Father. She turned her attention to everyone seated at the table, "Does that sound to anyone like too harsh a punishment for an unfortunate accident?"

"But it's what the damage is," Emily said, daring to look up and meet the eyes of her mother. "It's what it costs. You taught me to be responsible for the things I do. How am I not responsible for this?"

Mother pursed her lips. "Still, it seems—"

"I admire the girl's spirit," Coleridge said. "Not sure I'd have had that kind of guts when I was her age."

The Father sniffed and got up from his chair. "As it is written, 'whatsoever a man soweth, that shall he also reap.' Perhaps the children will be more careful in the future."

Coleridge's eyes met Mr. Tuttle's, and something passed between them. "Okay," Mr. Tuttle said. "Are we agreed?"

Emily nodded. Mom seemed reticent, but eventually she dipped her head as well.

"Then we'll handle it." Mr. Tuttle rose from his place and walked over by the Father. "You'll have insurance replace the window, and we'll pay you back. It may take some time."

Father MacGillivray said, "Let us know how you would like to pay, whether in regular payments or a lump sum." He said to Coleridge, "There won't be any need to press charges for criminal mischief. I think we can handle this among ourselves. Thank you for coming, officer."

Coleridge clicked his radio. "We're done here. I'll be out in a second." He nodded to the Father and said to the Tuttles, "Mind if I walk you out?"

The party gathered itself up and marched through the nave and out the front door.

Coleridge waved at his partner who was standing guard over the bikes and other things.

"Emily will have to get a job. That won't do her any harm," Mr. Tuttle said to Coleridge, shaking his hand.

"It won't, but I wish the money she earns would go to her college fund instead of that guy," he said, tossing his thumb back over his shoulder.

"You're not a religious fellow, I take it."

"Not that kind." He sketched a salute, and turned to Emily. "You're going places, young lady. This won't set you back, I promise."

"I hope you're right. Feels pretty low right now," she said.

"Bet it does. You've restored some of my faith in the future, though, I'll tell you that. If you don't get anything else out of it, you'll have a friend on the force from now on."

Mrs. Tuttle put her arm around her daughter. "I don't expect we'll need that, but thank you for being so kind, officer."

"Ma'am." He turned on his heel and walked back to his cruiser.

The Tuttles watched him go. "Well," Mr. Tuttle said, "this isn't quite how I thought this day would go."

Emily got on her bike and pedaled. That way, no one could see the tears on her cheeks. Ethan rode after her, keeping her in sight. He didn't have anything to say.

"Wait, I have to get a job, too?" Ethan said. "I didn't do anything wrong."

"Neither did your sister," Mrs. Tuttle said. "Don't tell me you wouldn't have hit that ball just as hard, if you could have."

"But... but... I was gonna—"

"Play on the X-box, yes, I know," Mrs. Tuttle said, stirring a pot on the stove. "You'll be able to. You'll just have to do it after you put some work in. You said yourself you didn't think it was fair that Emily had to pay for the window by herself. Now she won't have to."

Ethan's mouth dropped open. "I don't even get to keep the money?"

"Not all of it, no." Mrs. Tuttle turned to him, wooden spoon in hand. "Tell me what part of this is not fair. Convince me I'm making a mistake."

Ethan wanted to do that more than anything in the world. He just couldn't think of how. His mouth opened and closed but nothing came out.

"Right," Mrs. Tuttle said. "I'm glad you're signed up for the local debate club next year. This summer you'll need to help your sister. You were on the ballfield, too. It could just as easily have been you that hit that ball."

"But what are we going to do? We're fifteen. We can't drive."

"It is a puzzle," Mrs. Tuttle said. "But we're working on it. Your Dad and I know some people who might be able to help. It would be a lot better if you were sixteen, of course; you'd have a lot more options."

Ethan scowled. "Because there's something magic about me being six months older. All of a sudden I'm responsible, or something. Didn't kids used to be able to work if they wanted to?"

Mrs. Tuttle nodded. "They did. Some of them were forced to. Which is why the government made it illegal."

"That works out great for us now, doesn't it?" Ethan said, pushing back from his chair and standing up. "I don't mind working. I just wish it were easier to get a job. And that I didn't have to give up my money to pay for a window I didn't break."

"Think of how grateful your sister will be."

"Think of how she's gonna owe me forever."

"Think of how you live in my house for free, and all I ask is a kiss on the cheek every now and then."

Ethan smiled at that. "I'll think about it." He kissed her on the cheek as he went out.

Mr. Tuttle started by calling Uncle Ben to see if he had something. "I know you've got this YouTube news broadcast that's pretty popular. I'm sure putting the kids on camera again is not something you need, but I thought maybe you could use some legwork, research or something."

"It's funny you called," Uncle Ben said. "I happen to be working on something pretty big—at least, I think it's pretty big—in Malantown, just across the river."

"Could you use the twins?"

"I could, if I can have them right away. Sometimes teenagers can get things done that old fogies like me can't. I'm working out of an office on Compton Street, if you can get them there on Monday."

"You'd be working as interns for your Uncle Ben. Paid interns, though," Mr. Tuttle said. "He's willing to pay $15 an hour."

Emily's face, which had showed nothing but misery for days, brightened a little. "That's pretty good," she said. "A lot better than I was thinking."

"We're very lucky," Mr. Tuttle said, stabbing some peas with his fork. "Your uncle pays much better than market rates. It's almost as if he likes you or something."

"Half your earnings should probably go to pay for the window. The rest can go to charity and savings," Mrs. Tuttle said.

Ethan got halfway out of his chair. "Whaaaat! It's bad enough I have to give up half my money, but now I don't get to spend any of it?"

"Well your options are fairly limited since you spent all your past savings on your big trip," Mr. Tuttle said. "That's why having a rainy day fund—some savings always set aside—is a good idea."

"Besides, what did you want to spend your money on?" Mrs. Tuttle said, calmly slicing pot roast.

"I don't… I mean, there's lots of stuff. Gum. Video games. Pizza."

"You'll have some money for those things," Mr. Tuttle said. "When you want to buy something, we'll take the money out of savings and you can spend it. You just have to tell us what it is you want to buy."

"You don't trust me," Ethan said, slumping back into his chair and crossing his arms.

Mr. Tuttle looked placidly across the table at him. "Do you think we should?"

"Yes."

"Why?"

Ethan thought maybe a bite of pot roast would be better than answering that question. But Emily spoke up. "Because he didn't leave me. He came with me to the church even though he didn't have to. He's been... actually really nice even though this isn't his fault."

Mr. Tuttle pursed his lips. "That's a pretty convincing argument, actually. Okay, Ethan. How about you get five percent as walking-around money."

Ethan did some math in his head. "That's not very much money. Only like sixty, seventy cents an hour."

"For a forty hour week, that's still twenty-eight bucks," Mrs. Tuttle pointed out. "You planning to spend more money than that on nonsense?"

Ethan shrugged and smiled a little. "I don't know. A guy has to have the green to make the scene."

Mr. Tuttle choked on his peas. "Make a little bit smaller scene, then, please. But if Emily thinks you should have some cash, then that's good enough for me."

"What will we be doing?" Emily said.

"I don't know, exactly. Monday morning I'm to deposit you at his office on Compton Street, and he'll assign you your jobs then. He's bunking in with some kind of community action organization. They do research and public outreach on city projects."

"They work for the city?" Emily said, as if saying that left a bad taste in her mouth.

"They're not on the city payroll, if that's what you're asking."

"Sounds sketchy," Emily said.

"Sounds like twenty-eight dollars in my pocket," Ethan said, stabbing a hefty slice of beef and transferring it to his plate. "I'm in, whatever it is."

The office of Community for Real Progress lay halfway along a mostly-deserted industrial street on Compton Street in Malantown. The Tuttles pulled up in front at a quarter after eight, and Uncle Ben came right out to meet them. Gusty wind tossed an old newspaper down the empty sidewalk across the street. The parking meter in front of the building had been decapitated, stringy wires poking up out of the empty post, like a tall metal stalk of wheat. The wind smelled of smoke and dust.

"Nice place you have here," Mr. Tuttle said, looking the street up and down. Each window was defended by heavy iron bars, and a metal grating defended the front door, rather like a portcullis.

"It's cheap," Uncle Ben said, smiling broadly. "How are you two?"

"We're good," Emily said. "Maybe a little sad not to be spending summer vacation hanging out instead of working all day."

"What were you going to do? Play baseball? I heard that was the source of the problem in the first place."

"I don't want to talk about it," she said.

"Too bad," Uncle Ben said, "because baseball is one of the things that brings you down here to this lovely garden spot."

Ethan gave his uncle a hug. "What about baseball?"

Uncle Ben waved that question away. "Plenty of time for that," he said. "Thanks for bringing them down, brother."

"My pleasure," Mr. Tuttle said, getting back in the car. "You want me to come pick them up this afternoon?"

Uncle Ben shook his head. "I'll bring them home for you. I don't know how late we might be today. Lots of work to do, and not a lot of time to do it."

Mr. Tuttle sketched a wave and drove off. Every now and then, an older-model car trundled by down the pitted blacktop, but other than that, the street seemed deserted. Across the street, a ten-story building squatted behind a chain-link fence with a businesslike padlock on the gate. The front door was plywood festooned with tape warning everyone to keep out.

But inside Uncle Ben's building, the atmosphere was warm and welcoming. A cheery receptionist stood as they came in and extended a hand. "I'm Margot," she said, pearl-white teeth standing out in a brilliant smile. "Welcome to CRP."

"CRP sounds like it's inviting people to make fun of it," Ethan said.

"We just kick the crap out of them, and they leave us alone," Margot said. "It's a joke. CRP, just add an 'A'—"

"I get it," Ethan said. "You don't look like you think the joke is all that funny."

"None of them are when you hear them six times a day," she said, wheeling her chair back to a filing cabinet and tugging open the bottom drawer.

"Come on in, kids. We're back here," Uncle Ben said, leading them around Margot's desk, past a conference room on the left and a copier on the right. None of the walls were painted, just whitewashed over the drywall. Emily could see where the screws were driven in. Above them, all the wiring and piping lay open to view, right to the steel beams that held up the roof.

"Cozy," she said, as they walked into a modest office at the rear corner of the building, across from the bathroom.

"It's home," Uncle Ben said, moving to close the door behind them. "We don't need a lot of decoration. This is a workspace and storage area, more than anything. We get a lot of people in here when we do a mailing or a big project, but right now everyone's out, which is what we need to talk about."

With the door shut, every word he said seemed to be sucked into the wall, as if the sound of his voice was killed dead the second he spoke. On every wall was egg-crate padding, and the ceiling had thick foam layered over the drop panels.

"You record in here, don't you?" Ethan said.

Uncle Ben nodded. "It's not totally soundproof, but it's pretty close. With the door shut, it does the job."

"Sounds weird," Emily said, turning her head, trying to catch some kind of echo.

"You get used to it," Uncle Ben said, flipping open his laptop. "Now, let's talk about this project I'm working on. You already know that my show tends to go after places where the government is doing bad things and needs to be corrected."

Ethan picked up a small model car in the corner. "Is something like that happening here in Malantown?"

"That's what I'm trying to find out. Do you two know anything about the town history?"

The twins shook their heads.

"Okay, well, briefly, at one time, Malantown and Spoonerville were one town, spanning the river. About thirty years ago, the towns divided, and since then Malantown has grown quite a bit larger than Spoonerville."

"Not to mention richer," Ethan said. He folded his arms across his chest.

Uncle Ben got a funny look on his face. "You'd think that, wouldn't you, with the fancy buildings downtown and the minor-league baseball and basketball teams."

"Which we don't have," Emily said.

"Right. But what if I told you looks can be deceiving?"

The twins exchanged a glance. This was getting good.

Uncle Ben saw it and nodded. "The baseball park is about twenty years old now, and there are plans to build another one, much larger, even though the team has been losing money for years. On the heels of that, the city is planning something bigger, something that has the whole town buzzing. They want to host the World Amateur Baseball Tournament here."

Emily sat up straight. "The world tournament? In Malantown? Where are they going to play the games? Surely not in Walter Piggott Stadium."

"Yes, there, but also in a new park with another three-field annex that seats almost as many as the Big Pig."

Ethan goggled. "Four new stadiums? Where on earth are they going to put them?"

"And how are they going to pay for them?" Emily said.

"Bingo," said Uncle Ben, sitting back in his chair and putting his hands behind his head. "That's the hundred-million-dollar question. As to where, that part is simple. They're putting them on the waterfront." A tiny smile lit his face as he watched the twins work things out.

"Along the river," Ethan said, sitting down next to his sister.

"But that's... right here," Emily said. "Compton Street is a block away from the river."

"There are already buildings here," Ethan said. "I mean, a lot of them are empty, but there's not much free land between the river and, what, a half mile away? How big are these places going to be?"

Emily screwed up her face, "With parking? Half mile, easy." She whistled. "That's a lot of real estate."

Uncle Ben's smile widened. "Want to see how much?"

Without waiting for an answer, he rolled his chair back and grabbed a cardboard cylinder from a barrel in the corner of the office. He uncapped it and drew out a large rolled-up sheet which he spread on the desk. They stood around it and Uncle Ben pointed. "Right here," he said, "is this office. All along here," he drew his finger down Compton Street, "we have offices that are more or less unoccupied. That's true here as well." He pointed to another street, Korver, that ran along the river.

"Nobody's going to miss those buildings if they knock them down, though I can't imagine how much it would cost to buy them all. Anyway, that's not the point, or at least it's not why I got out this map. The proposed site of one of the new stadia would take all this out, but the other complex, more of a set of fields than a single stadium, is proposed to go right here." He stabbed his index finger down on a cluster of buildings on the south end of Compton, where the river made a right turn and the street dead ended. "And this part of town is a lot different than where we are now, even though it's only just down the street a quarter mile."

"That's not an office block, is it?" Ethan said.

"No. It's not."

"Houses. Those are houses, aren't they?" Emily said, eyes on the map.

"They are. Not very nice ones, I'll grant you, but houses nonetheless. Stacked together, old, small, drafty, and no doubt leaky when it rains. There's a lot of crime in that area, and the streets are dirty. But they're houses, all right, and getting the rights to bulldoze them isn't likely, unless the price is far more than they'll be willing to pay."

"Eminent domain," Emily said. "We know

all about what cities do when they want a piece of property and can't get anyone to sell at a market price."

Uncle Ben said, "That part is done. There's nothing we can do about it. But we might be able to stop the bulldozers with some creativity." He rolled the map back up and slid it into its tube. "The attack is two-pronged. One has to do with research at the city archives, looking through the history of the town and a lot of dusty city council meeting notes. The other involves going into that neighborhood and interviewing people. The government said the area was blighted because of crime and decaying houses. But I have a hunch there is more good stuff going on down there than anyone wants to admit. I need proof."

"Can we each choose one?" Ethan said.

"No," said Uncle Ben. "I can't send one of you in there alone, so whatever you do, you do it together."

"Well," Emily said to Ethan, "What would you rather do?"

If you think they should go to the archives, turn to page 104.

If you think they should go to the neighborhood, turn to page 144.

It was no use. You could fool some of the people all of the time, and all of the people some of the time, but Mom always found out. It was so true, Mom had it in vinyl lettering on the door leading out to the garage. Emily could keep trying to hide it, keep pretending like it didn't matter, like the window was someone else's fault, but she knew it wasn't. Emily was responsible. Time to start acting like she was responsible.

"Mom," she started to say, when Mom's phone rang.

"Hang on," Mom said, punching the dashboard answer button. "Hello."

"Mrs. Tuttle, this is Detective Goldstein. I'd like to come and see you for a moment, if you're going to be home this afternoon."

"I don't think we have anything to discuss, detective, but if you really need to, I'll be pulling into my driveway in two minutes, and you'd be welcome any time after that."

"Thank you. I really won't take much of your time, but I think there's something we should discuss. I'll see you in a few minutes."

He hung up. "Huh," Mom said. "I wonder what that's about."

"It's about me," Emily said. Her breath choked. She couldn't say anything. All her energy was needed to keep her burning eyes from spilling over.

"About you?" The car slowed and Emily heard gravel under the tires. Mom put it in park and kept her eyes on the front windshield. "Whatever you did, Emily, no matter what it is, I'm your mother, and I will be. Always. You'll have my support and my love in spite of anything."

"But you… want me to tell you. What happened."

"Of course I do, but that's not the most important thing. The most important thing is that you, Emily Tuttle, are loved for who and what you are. You have a good heart and a good head. I love you and nothing will change that."

And she said nothing more. Just sat there, looking out the window.

Emily couldn't help it. She buried her head in her hands and a wracking sob broke through her resolve.

Then Mom moved. She laid a warm hand on Emily's shoulder and drew her over toward her, wrapping her in the kind of embrace Emily couldn't remember receiving since she was a small child. It was familiar and safe, and it broke her resolve completely. For long moments, all she could do was cry.

"It was me," Emily finally choked out.

"What was?" Mom's voice was gentle.

"The window. At the church. I broke it."

"You said you didn't."

"I know!" she wailed. "I was so scared. The police and everything. I didn't mean to. I didn't think I could hit a ball that far. I didn't think anyone could hit a ball that far. But then I hit it and it went through the window. At first it wasn't so bad, just one chunk, but then the whole thing came crashing down and I didn't know what to do so I ran. And then I couldn't say anything. I couldn't tell you."

Mom let her talk and her tale ran down into tears again, but these tears were cleansing and not quite so burdened by guilt.

"So now what do I do?" Emily said, when she'd had a moment to let her sobs subside.

"What do you think we should do?"

Emily looked stricken. She had thought Mom would just tell her. She didn't want to think about it. Besides, could she tell the police now that she had broken the window, after telling them she hadn't?

"The policeman..."

"Yes, he's waiting at our house, I believe."

"He'll arrest me."

Mom allowed just the hint of a smile. "No, I don't think he'll arrest you."

"But, if I tell, what will happen?"

Mom pursed her lips. "I don't know. It's hard to say about things like this. But I think you have to understand—you've already told. You told me. I can't just ignore that. But I'm not going to take the decision away from you. You have to decide what you want to do."

Emily sat for a long time, staring out the window. "It was an accident. I can say that. I didn't mean to break it, I just hit a ball really well. No one can blame me for that."

"No, they can't."

This gave Emily some confidence. Now that she was talking about it, it wasn't so hard. "The window is really expensive, but the thing that makes it expensive is that it's so old and it's kind of an heirloom, kind of like a town mascot or something. The window can be put right, and even though it won't be exactly the same as it was, it can probably be pretty close, so no one can tell. I'm sure they're going to want like a hundred thousand dollars for it, but it's not fair to make me pay that."

"What would be fair?"

"I can't answer that, I don't think. But I think it would be fair to ask me to pay to replace the window, to put it back the way it was, as close as we can get." Emily turned her face up to her mother's. "Does that sound right?"

"It sounds fair to me."

Mom started the car again and slowly rolled back out onto the road.

The policeman greeted them with a somber face but agreed to allow Emily to tell him her story. Through it all, he said nothing, just watched her face and listened. In the end he sighed, but it was a sigh of contentment and not frustration. He reached into his bag. "I'm glad you told me," he said, and drew out a round white object. "Because we found this."

It was the baseball. In tiny letters along one seam were the initials ET.

Emily reached out for it and rolled it off the detective's hand. It dropped into her palm. On one side was a mark, like an oval bruise. She laid her finger along it and smiled sadly. "It really was the sweetest hit."

"Must have been," the detective said. "One reason we didn't suspect you at first was that the wall of the church is almost 500 feet away from home plate. That's a serious major-league wallop you gave this thing. We didn't really think any of you kids could hit a ball that far. But then we found the baseball and that pretty much told us the story."

He shifted in his seat. "The only question was whether you did it on purpose or whether it was an accident."

"It was, I swear it—"

The detective laid his hand on the ball. "You don't have to convince me. I made a couple of calls, and everyone agreed that Emily Tuttle would never have done such a thing on purpose. Quite a few people, however, believed in your hitting skills. And I don't know a lot about teenage girls but I do know a true story when I hear one. Don't worry, Miss Tuttle. No one is going to jail here."

"I'm willing to pay. I got a job."

This time the look on the policeman's face was harder to read. Emily thought there might be some pain in it. "That's very noble of you. I don't know what the church is going to want you to do."

"Whatever it is," Mom said, re-entering the conversation, "we're prepared to do it. All of us."

"That's good. I'll let them know. Probably you'll need to have a meeting with them. They won't be pleased that you didn't come forward sooner, you know," he said to Emily, "and it would certainly have been a lot better if you had."

Emily hung her head. Detective Goldstein stood and shook Mom's hand. Emily rose and held hers out as well. "I'm proud of you for finally coming forward," he said. "That took courage."

"Not enough," Emily said, in a small voice.

The detective excused himself and Mom shut the door behind him. Ethan bounded down the stairs. "So, did she fess up?"

Mom fixed him with a hard stare. "You knew about this, I assume."

Ethan stopped short. Maybe this wasn't a good time to get involved. "I… Yeah, well, I was there when it happened, but Emily kept saying it didn't, that it couldn't have—"

"But you knew it did."

Ethan's face lost some color. "Well… I mean, I promised I wouldn't tell. I didn't do anything. I was just on second base."

"You were playing baseball on the same field as your sister, and you'll share whatever happens to her."

"That's not fair!"

"It most certainly is not. Emily's only crime was doing something really well. It seems like she shouldn't be punished for that."

"She did lie about it."

Mom smiled triumphantly. "She's not the only one, is she?"

Ethan's mouth dropped open.

Mom patted him on the shoulder. "Don't worry. The detective says no one is going to be arrested. So you'll probably get off with having to pay for the window. It could be worse."

No one was arrested, but the church elders were plenty steamed about their window having been smashed and then run away from. It did not show "proper remorse" they said, that the confession came only after the police had procured evidence that would have identified the guilty party. Never mind that the confession came before the evidence was produced. That cut no ice. They wanted blood, and in the end, they got it.

The window itself could be replaced for $15,000 or thereabouts, but the sentimental value, not to mention the desire for punitive damages, drove the price a good deal higher. It was that or a charge of criminal vandalism, which neither Ethan nor Emily were prepared to refute. After all, if it had truly been an accident, why hadn't they come forward at the time? No, running away was evidence that they were guilty, because as the Good Book says, only the guilty flee when no man pursues.

"There would have been plenty of pursuit," Ethan grumbled, but only when he and Emily were alone.

The eventual total cost was $31,000. Mom and Dad came up with half—Dad borrowed against his retirement—which mollified the church elders a bit, and Emily and Ethan had to come up with the rest. Never mind the replacement cost—Carla had been dead right after all—what mattered was the price the elders felt they were due for having to make do with a replacement window. They had originally wanted much more, as much as $100,000, a figure that included "lost revenue from tourism," as if the church made any money off the tourists.

"Donations," they sniffed, "which will now be denied us forever because of your thoughtlessness."

Emily had no answer to that.

She did go back to the Chicken Shack; she had no choice. Not just that summer, but throughout her adolescence, she worked there as often as she could, managing a busy schedule pursuing other opportunities. It took three years of saving every penny for her to save up enough money to pay off the debt on the window. Ethan was also forced to contribute. He got a paper route and also worked for a local construction firm carrying lumber to the framing crew. It was a terrible job, hot in the summer, freezing in winter, but what could he do?

"It's indentured servitude, is what it is," he said one day at the table.

"Except there's no contract," Emily said. Her mood was foul. Wasn't doing the right thing supposed to make you happier?

"There's a contract, all right," Mom said. "I can show it to you. And considering we liquidated a good chunk of our retirement to be able to pay off half of it, I think bellyaching is the last thing you should think about."

Emily hung up her cleats, her mitt, and her bat, and never played again. It wasn't the end of the world. But some days, it felt like it.

THE END

"We should think about what is consistent with what we've done before," Ethan said. "It's like a brand. We're loud, we're in your face, so we should keep that up. It's working."

"Or we could change our messaging and try to get more people involved," Emily said.

Uncle Ben said, "I once heard a wise man say, 'You can't make friends of your enemies by making enemies of your friends.' I think that applies in this case. If I were going to cast a vote, I'd be all for Ethan's plan. I think it's best to keep playing to the strengths we've demonstrated so far."

"I'd like to see if my plan would work, but I'm feeling like a little yelling and screaming, too. If it will settle us, I'll vote for Ethan, and we can get started."

Ethan's mouth dropped open. "Really?" he said. "You're siding with my idea?"

"Sure. I'll make you pay for it later, but when you're right, you're right. What do we do first?"

The three of them planned the rest of that day, looking at the probable assembly area for the incoming delegation, how they could best present themselves in annoying areas, and what kind of amplification they thought they could get away with.

"One more thing," Uncle Ben said, tipped back in his chair and looking at the ceiling. "We need to talk to the city. For something like this we'll need a permit."

"Free speech," Ethan said. "We should be able to say anything we want."

"And assembly," Emily said. "That's the first amendment to the Constitution. Congress shall make no law, and so on."

Uncle Ben picked up a broom and picked at the dust in the corner. "Malantown is not governed by 'Congress shall make no law.' Besides, the Supreme Court has ruled several times that cities may restrict where and in what manner people may protest."

Emily retrieved the dustpan and crouched where Uncle Ben could sweep into it. "Wait, is this the 'free speech zone' thing?"

"Never heard of that," Ethan said.

"It's where the city designates a place for protesting, so if you want to hold a protest, you can do it, but you can't do it just anywhere. The city says what areas are okay and what are not. Like, if there's an economic summit or something, and people want to get in the faces of the diplomats, they can't, because the city has a free speech zone set up a couple blocks away."

"Where are the free speech zones in Malantown?" Ethan said. Uncle Ben swept up dark brown dust and a couple of stray Cheetos, and Emily dumped them in the can.

"No idea. I wouldn't be surprised if they'd never had to figure that out. I'm not going to ask about that, I'm just going to apply for a permit to protest," Uncle Ben said.

Emily racked the dustpan and sat down. "But even that—isn't there something wrong with that? If I have to ask the city for a permit to do something, isn't the city the one that has power over whether I can do it? So, do my free speech rights come from the city now? I thought those were some of the unalienable ones."

"It's complicated," Uncle Ben said. "Maybe it would be easier if we went outside. I can show you some things."

Blessedly, clouds blocked the sun for a moment, otherwise the day would have been sweltering. As it was, sweat beaded up on Ethan's forehead the second he stepped outside. Uncle Ben grabbed a patch of shade under a scraggly tree and waited for the twins to join him.

When they did, he pointed down the street. "Okay, first off, what we have is a conflict of rights. Who has the right to walk down the sidewalk?"

Emily said, "I do. I mean, we all do. Anyone. The sidewalk is a public place."

"Okay. What about the street?"

Ethan screwed up his face. "The street is the same, isn't it? A public place?"

"So I can walk right out into the middle of it?"

"If you're stupid."

"Let's say I am. I walk out into the street. A car comes along. Who has the right to be there?"

"The car does," Ethan said. "But, you do too, I think. I'm not sure."

Uncle Ben nodded. A car obligingly passed by, the occupants wondering at the little group watching them from the sidewalk. "This is a conflict of rights, you could say. Both of us have a right to be there. But the car has the superior right, based on the rules that have been set up for roads. If I get in the way and get hit, it's probably my fault. I'll be the one that gets the ticket, even if there's no collision."

"That sounds fair, I guess. But what does that have to do with our protest?"

A man walked by with his daughter. "Howdy," he said.

"Harya," said Uncle Ben. "That fellow there with his daughter. He has the right to be on the sidewalk, you said. What if I'm already there?"

"He has to move around you."

"What if there are so many of us that he can't do that?"

Ethan got it. "Like with the protest. I get it. If we put so many people on the sidewalk that we're blocking it, then it's like the car thing. People need to walk down the sidewalk, and if we're there they can't do it. So that wouldn't be okay."

"But do you need a permit to be on the sidewalk?"

"Well, no, I don't think so. Here we are and we didn't have to ask anyone about it."

"That's right. You can say pretty much anything you want on the sidewalk, because you have the right to be there. You can even hand people a pamphlet or a flyer if you want to, though of course you can't make them take it."

"But we want to do something more aggressive than that," Emily said. "We want signs and noise and all sorts of things. We probably want to block the street, don't we?"

"And if we do?"

"We will need a permit. That makes sense. We have the right to be there on the street, but the cars have the superior right, so we need a permit if we're going to be in their space."

Uncle Ben smiled. "Bingo. What about noise?"

"We're gonna make some," Ethan said. "A lot of it."

"Is that a right? Do you have the right to make noise?"

"Sure. I'm making noise right now."

"What if I don't like the noise you're making? Do I have the right to be free of your noise?"

Emily shook her head. "Sometimes I wish I had the right to be free of his noise."

"But you do, actually, in some circumstances. Suppose he's bugging you at home."

"Mom puts a stop to it."

"Because Mom is the owner. That's private property, and she holds the rights to it. But what about out here?"

Ethan stepped out onto the sidewalk and kicked at a weed growing through the cracks. "I don't know. I don't think you can get on a guy for talking to you. Like you were saying, I have the right to be here."

"What about if I'm yelling?"

Ethan shrugged. "It depends."

"On?"

"What you're yelling. If it's mean or dangerous or something, that interferes with my right to be on the sidewalk. And you can't have a bullhorn, either, or, I don't know, drums or something. You can only make so much noise before it starts to bruise other people's rights."

Uncle Ben pointed up at the windows above. "What about those people?"

Emily shaded her eyes. Even with the clouds, it was plenty bright. "Those people have private homes, so they have private property rights. You can't make too much noise or that infringes on their rights."

"So if I'm going to have a bullhorn—"

"And you definitely are, for our protest."

"—Then I need a permit. I need permission."

Emily counted in her head. "There are like thirty homes just in this building. You can't get permission from all of them."

Uncle Ben shook his head. "Those people delegate their right to police that to the city, and the city is the one that issues the permission to make that kind of noise. So it's not quite as simple as 'I have free speech' or 'I have freedom of assembly.' Other people have rights, too, and those rights have to be respected."

"Freedom is messy," Ethan said, picking up a loose rock. "I have the right to throw this rock, but I don't have the right to smash that car window with it. I guess

I kind of get the idea of why the city should be able to issue permits, as long as they do it fairly."

"That's always the problem, isn't it?" Emily said. "They should have to give a permit to anyone for anything, as long as they're observing the rules. But I bet they won't like our protest. They might not be too excited to give us a permit for it."

"Then we'll make do with what we have the right to do anyway, staying on the sidewalks and keeping the noise down."

"What about free speech zones?" Emily said, her eyes measuring distance down toward the end of the street.

"Those are for larger events, the kind that could disrupt the city traffic in unacceptable ways—so, for instance, if you're going to block half of downtown, the city will have to put you someplace less disruptive to other people's rights."

"Which is kind of like shutting you up," Ethan said, face set hard.

"It can be, yes. I won't say that cities aren't sometimes pretty arbitrary about how they do permitting and such, but it's not quite as simple as it might look at first."

Emily started walking toward the river. "I think we need to figure out exactly what we're asking for. Let's take a close look at the block and make a plan so we know what we're asking the city for."

"And then we can make a backup plan for when the city says no," Ethan said, following in her wake. "Just in case."

The city did not say no. But the permit took a long time to get and didn't get issued until the day before the visit from the International Baseball Committee.

"Typical," Ethan said. "We're hardly in their way at all, and everyone who might be bothered by the noise is already a part of the protest."

Mrs. Douglass, however, had not been idle. She canvassed the entire neighborhood, talking to everyone and getting people ready. "We'll be out there anyway, permit or no permit, so we might as well have our game ready to go."

And they did.

A sea of faces poured from the buildings, and from neighboring streets they gathered by the hundreds, signs in hand. Their faces were grim, but their steps determined.

More people began to show up who surely didn't live in the neighborhood. Parking as many as four blocks away, people showed up from other parts of Malantown, and even from Spoonerville. People of all races and classes came out to support the protest, it seemed.

"We don't want to block the street," a dynamo named Carol said, directing traffic through her bullhorn, standing on a wooden box in the middle of the street. "We want to line it, thick on each side. Pick a block. They're going to come down Fulton and make a right at Riverside. We need people all along there. You got chant sheets?" she shouted, waving a sheaf of papers. Choruses of "no" cascaded around the block. Carol handed a thick stack to Emily and another one to Ethan. "Go get 'em," she said. "Get these things out there." The big woman's smile flashed out like sunshine. "Just like old times," she said. "I love this stuff."

Mrs. Douglass had found Carol right down on the last building of the street on the top floor, a grandma to four little kids. When Carol heard what they were planning, her eyes lit up. "I used to do that when I was a kid in college," she said. "Nothing like a good old protest."

She proved to have fantastic organizational skills, plus a voice like a freight train horn. People did what she said. People could hear what she said, bullhorn or no. With a bullhorn, it was like hearing a voice from Heaven.

Uncle Ben checked his phone and tapped Carol on the leg. "They've landed at the airport. They should be here in less than an hour."

The smile blazed out again. "We'll be ready. Oh, Lord, will we be ready."

They kept the streets empty—well, as empty as those Malantown streets ever were—until the motorcade with the baseball delegation turned right onto

Fulton. Ethan, videoing the proceedings, wondered what that must have been like, cruising calmly along, then turning right and into a maelstrom of noise and chaos.

It was hard to know how many people came out in response to the pleas they made in person and on social media, but it was far more than they had planned on, and almost more than they could use.

Carol, though, smiled everyone into position and kept them relatively quiet until showtime.

And what a show it was.

They had the permit to block off Fulton and Riverside for two blocks for the protest, but they hadn't had much time to set up how that would look, and blocking those streets would have given the city hosts a place they could be sure to avoid. So they didn't block the streets at all. They left them open. But they lined them as thick and deep as they had people for, and when the car turned and started down the street, they let loose a howl that shook the city.

Every face in all three cars was turned to look at the hordes that dominated every inch of sidewalk and out a few feet into the street. Each group had a leader buried in it, and the leader would call out the chants, almost like a soccer fan club in a stadium ("Actually, they stole it from us," Carol said with a wink). The coordination wasn't perfect, but it was very good. You could hear "Hey hey, Ho ho, people yes and baseball no" all the way downtown.

The protest was loud enough that when the delegation stopped at its designated spot, where the city hosts were going to get out and stand looking at the area to talk about what they envisioned and relating the vision of what Malantown could be as a host for the baseball tournament, they had to move off to a much less desirable location because of the noise. Trash littered the ground they moved to, and more, they were in clear view of the apartment buildings that were to be demolished. The protest group had hung huge banners from the rear windows, saying things like "Thank you for throwing us out at home" and "Your home for a day, our homes gone forever."

"It had to be really uncomfortable," Ethan said, reviewing his videos. "You can see it on the footage that they kept looking around, listening to what we were saying."

The climax came when Carol took the microphone just as the delegation was returning to their vehicles carrying glasses of champagne. Her already-powerful voice was amplified by two huge sound systems, and the street was choked with every protestor, roaring approval at everything she said.

She delivered a stemwinder, too, a terrific speech that had the crowd howling, laughing, cheering their lungs out. "When God led the Israelites out of Egypt, He took them to the Promised Land," she bellowed. "This is hardly the land flowing with milk and honey,"

she said, to general laughter, "but this is our home. And when Elisha showed his servant the armies of the Lord, they filled the valley in defiance of the enemy. Today, we defy the city, we defy the world, for they that are with us are more than they that are with them!"

"That was incredible," Emily said, sitting in front of a special at the local ice cream shop. "The hair on my arms is still standing up."

"It was worth it even if we lose," Ethan said.

Uncle Ben tallied the traffic online and pronounced the whole enterprise a nuclear success. "I've never had anything like this before," he said. "We're going to have real impact with this stuff."

"Will it be enough?" Ethan said.

"Impossible to know. But if it isn't, we couldn't have done anything that would have been."

Uncle Ben opened his office for the online broadcast of the announcement of the venue for the International Baseball Tournament. People from the neighborhood packed the place, hopeful but resigned. Carol came, and Mrs. Douglass, and DeShaun and Reggie from across the street, and a couple dozen others. Uncle Ben projected the announcement onto the big white wall, and they stood around drinking soda and eating chips until the chairman approached the podium.

Uncle Ben held up his hands for quiet. "Before he starts, can I just thank all of you for your hard work to give us a chance at this thing? I'm so grateful for all you did."

Mrs. Douglass spoke up from the back. "And we thank you, sir, and your great kids, for taking this as more than a job. You made it a cause, and you didn't have to. Y'all have your homes, but you went all the way to help us stay in ours. Me and mine, we won't forget that."

The video sharpened and the Chairman of the IBC stepped to the microphone. "We at the IBC have given the decision about the next international baseball tournament much thought. We had many worthy competitors. But in the end, one city stood above the others, and will host the upcoming tournament."

Emily gave Carol a hug. "Win or lose, we're with you."

"Sugar, we can't lose. We can only be moved to fight another day."

The video showed a short movie, and the name of the winning city came up. Kyoto, Japan.

For a moment, silence reigned. Then the crowd blew the top off the building with cheering. DeShaun ran out of the building screaming, "We did it! We did it!" running down the street. Right down the middle, permit or no.

The group poured outside into the late afternoon sunshine, looking at the neighborhood with new eyes. Backslapping, hugging, crying, the residents melted down the street with tears on their faces and hope in their eyes.

When they were gone, Uncle Ben turned to the kids.

"You know, just because they didn't get the tournament doesn't mean they won't still try to knock all this down. We won this battle, but we could still lose the war."

But Emily shook her head. "We can't lose," she said. "We can only be moved. And this time, they're not moving us."

The End

Since Mom often had really interesting things going on, Emily was sure that the best course for her was to take the offer to work with her.

Mom took the news stoically, barely looking up from her book when Emily told her.

Ethan shook his head and made a face. "I don't think you've thought this through," he said. "Working for someone else, there's only so much they can do to you. Working for Mom? I think the law says she can work you 20 hours a day and pay you sixteen cents."

"It does not."

"Okay, it doesn't. But it probably doesn't say anything at all, and that's almost worse."

"It's going to be fine," Emily said, and shut her door and went to bed, but before she dropped off to sleep she wondered if Ethan hadn't been right. Mom loved her, yes. But she also had a different idea about what loving her daughter meant than sometimes Emily would have preferred.

And so it proved, almost before the sun was up the next morning.

Mom burst through the door while it was still too dark to see and before Emily could roll over to say "Mom, what the what?" Mom pulled from her pocket a canned air horn and blew a blast to wake the dead.

Emily vaulted out of bed as if it were on fire. She stood in the middle of the spiral-woven rug, chest heaving, eyes splayed wide with the whites showing.

"Up and at 'em," Mom said, as cheerfully as if they'd been sitting down to brunch. And she left without another word.

"Mom!" Emily cried after her, but there was no response.

Emily thought the best revenge would be to go back to bed, but there was more chance of her sprouting wings and flying than falling asleep after that wakeup call, so she sat down on the bed and started peeling off her pajamas.

Mom stuck her head in. "Five minutes," she said. "Meet me in the kitchen."

"What are we—" Emily began, but Mom's head was gone again.

She realized she didn't know what to wear. An evil thought crossed her mind, and she was in no condition to resist it.

Four minutes later, Emily sauntered into the kitchen wearing a bathing suit and flip-flops, with a smile on her face that said, "two can play this game."

And perhaps two could, but one of the two was considerably better at it than the other.

Mom, far from being crestfallen, as Emily hoped, smiled her best and said, "Wonderful! Right on time. There's toast in the toaster and butter on the block. If you want something more substantial, you'll have to get up earlier. We have to be out of here in another five minutes, so there's no time to cook anything."

Emily sort of spun in place, showing off her outfit as nonchalantly as possible. Maybe Mom just hadn't processed it yet. Surely she couldn't mean to have Emily actually stay in this outfit. In public. If they were going to be in public. Emily realized she knew nothing at all about what she was going to be doing.

But Mom didn't rise to the bait. Didn't even give it a nibble. "Toast is getting cold," she said, and peeled the lid off a yogurt.

The toast was already cold and wouldn't melt the butter. Stiff and dry, the slice of bread just lay there like a piece of cardboard. Emily remembered she had a hard-boiled egg in the fridge. She retrieved it and began to tap it on the counter to break up the shell.

"One minute," Mom said, breezing back in from somewhere. "I'll be in the car. If you're not there, I'll leave you."

Emily had another wicked idea, but the first one hadn't gone well, so she shoved it down and grabbed a plastic bag, dumped salt into it, and scampered out the garage door.

Mom's car was clearing the garage and backing down the driveway.

It hadn't even been close to a minute. Emily was sure of it. She jogged down the pavement and grabbed the passenger door handle as the garage door lowered behind her.

Throwing herself into her seat, she glared at her mother. "What is all this?" she said. "You're leaving me?"

"I would have," Mom said, again with that nauseatingly cheerful voice. "I have places to be. I need you to be there with me."

"Or what?" Emily said, defiance ringing through her voice.

"Or you'll be packed off to work with cousin Abraham's roofing company."

Emily stared. That was worse than anything she could have imagined. It made working at MacBurger or the Chicken Shack sound like, well, like summer vacation. Which is what this was supposed to be, Emily realized. What a nightmare. This had to be the worst summer in the history of ever. It was more of an un-summer, instead of anything feeling like a vacation or break.

"He won't hire me. I can't do that work. It will kill me."

"Possibly. It has been known to happen, although Abe is very conscientious about safety."

"MOM! I don't even like climbing ladders to change a light bulb!"

"Something to get over, it seems to me. Nevertheless, here you are, charmingly attired, and you have thus spared me a phone call and a plane ticket. Eat your toast."

"It's dry."

"Really? Huh. I wouldn't have guessed the toaster would do that."

Mom was apparently going to be snotty, so Emily responded as best she could by eating her egg in hostile and increasingly apprehensive silence. If this was how the day's appetizer tasted, what would the main course taste like?

She found out about twenty minutes later. Mom pulled into the parking lot of the local golf course and parked at the far end, about sixteen miles from the clubhouse. She reached down and popped the trunk. "We'll need to carry some things in."

"Some things."

"Yes, some things."

"Like golf clubs?"

"Oh, we're not playing," Mom said. "We have another task today."

In the trunk, four cardboard boxes lay nestled in a huge multicolored quilt. Mom draped the quilt over Emily and handed her a box. She took one under each arm and left the trunk open. As they turned, a golf cart ran up behind them and a garden gnome ejected himself and bowed.

"Madame Tuttle. And Mademoiselle Tuttle, I presume." Not actually a garden gnome, then, but a wizened little man with a bald head and a beard, anyway. Possibly a garden gargoyle. Or one of the sprites of the golf course who moved your ball when you weren't looking.

"Goofer. Glad to see you. There's a couple more boxes in the trunk, could you get those?"

"With the greatest pleasure," Goofer said, and whipped the boxes out of the trunk and into the cart's capacious backside. "And now, if you ladies would like to climb aboard my magic carpet, I shall deliver you to the festivities *tout suite*."

Mom acted like this was entirely normal behavior, and maybe it was. She closed the trunk, hit the lock on the key fob, and was rewarded by a sullen chirp from the car. She climbed into the front bench next to Goofer and left the back seat for Emily.

The cart zoomed off, picking up speed as the electric motor cut in. The sun had barely begun to threaten the eastern horizon, but the birds were hard at work, and more people, walking toward the clubhouse, waved at the travelers. It seemed a very odd parade.

Halfway to the clubhouse, Goofer turned around and extended a hand to Emily. "I'm Andrew Guffrain, popularly known as Goofer. You may address me as 'Your Highness.' And you are?"

Emily wasn't sure whether to take the man's hand or not. If he had actual flesh and bones, would that make this dream actually be happening?

"Emily Tuttle," she said, deciding that to not shake was rude. He squeezed her hand with his deceptively frail-looking hand, not painfully, but enough that she could tell he was much stronger than he looked.

Goofer looked at Mom. "She's in for a treat today! Did you have a specific assignment in mind for her?"

"Nothing in particular. I thought she could generally do whatever needed doing."

Goofer was horrified. "In that outfit? Good heavens no. By the power of Grayskull, she must attend my post and assist with the most complicated, the most daring, the most challenging of all the events on the course today! She is made for the adventure! It is kismet! Fate, I tell you."

Mom shrugged. "If you're sure. She's a good worker, though a little out of sorts today."

"Need your beauty sleep, eh?" he said, back over his shoulder. "Time for work! Time for service! Time to make all the other booths pale and shiver in comparison."

Emily could make sense out of none of this. She peeked in one of the boxes and found it filled to the brim with yellow rubber ducks. That figured. None of this was real. It couldn't be. This was some sort of tortured nightmare. If she went along with it for a while, she'd wake up and go down to breakfast, where there would be bacon. That was the only thing to do.

"I'm happy to help," Emily said, pasting on a smile. "That's what I came for."

"That's the spirit!" said the gnome—Emily had decided he was a gnome after all—and whizzed up the ramp to the wide brownstone-and-wood clubhouse with its panoramic view of the golf course. He jerked to a stop right in front of the main doors, where a host of tables stood, partially loaded with an assortment of goods—blankets, boom boxes, laptops, iPads, quilts, sleeves of golf balls, keychains, car emergency tool sets, and too many other things to keep track of. A huge banner hung lazily from the front overhang by three of its four grommets, so that right now it read "lf Tournament".

Gangs of people bustled in and out of the clubhouse doors, picking things up off the tables according to no discernible pattern and carrying them inside, then returning from inside with another armful of similar things to replace them.

"Good!" said a tallish woman with short red hair and the smallest waist Emily had ever seen. "You're here. Goofer, your mission is to go back out to the parking lot and retrieve any stragglers. Leave no soldier behind."

Goofer saluted smartly and sprang back into his cart. He whisked off around the side of the building and was gone.

The wasp-waisted woman hugged Mom with her free arm. "Good to see you," she said. "How are you this morning?"

"Wonderful! So excited. This is my daughter Emily," she said.

"Amelia Zuerlein," the woman said, nodding rather than extending a hand. "Everyone calls me Zoo. Which is what this place is going to be in five minutes. We've got a long way to go." She looked about in some indecision, then saw the banner. Her face fell. "That silly thing…" Her eyes lit on Emily. "Back of that bush there is a ladder. Will you cinch that stupid banner back in place, please? There's a hook up on the gutter, but the rope must have come undone again. Thank you, that's a big help." To Mom she said, "Everything on that table there has to come inside so we can use the table for registration. Can you get it?"

Mom said she could, and wrapped her arms around the heap of quilts, carrying them off in Zoo's wake. Neither of them so much as looked back to see if Emily were going to do the thing she had been asked to do.

The ladder was tall. Emily was wearing flip-flops and not a lot else. Men and women rushed by her like a river split by a rock and didn't pay her the slightest attention. But the banner hung there, crying out for attention. Emily hiked up her suit and went to find the ladder.

A rope ran from the grommet out to the side, frayed at the end. Emily squinted up at the gutter. A couple inches from the edge of the roof, a piece of rope dangled, similarly frayed. The knot had held, but the rope had given way. Emily couldn't tell if there was enough left to secure the banner. There was only one way to know for sure, and it involved climbing the ladder.

Up in the air, in front of everyone, working on the banner that was the first thing everyone would see when they came up from the parking lot to the club-house. Emily closed her eyes and couldn't understand why the nightmare wasn't coming to an end yet. Could it get worse?

It could. She mounted the ladder and climbed, her eyes up, not wanting to look down. It couldn't be more than a few feet. Not much more than she was tall. She could do that. Piece of cake.

The rope had broken close enough to the gutter-hook that she thought she might get the banner up without needing to get a new rope. Tying a slipknot in the end of the banner side of the rope, she tugged the broken piece off the gutter and stretched out the remaining rope to get it hooked.

No good. The rope was a couple inches too short. Emily pulled hard, but there just wasn't enough of it.

"Not going to make it, is it?" said a voice from below.

Emily looked down into a pair of dark brown eyes framed by freckles and curly blonde hair.

And fell off the ladder.

She was right. It wasn't far. But it was far enough to be embarrassing beyond all comprehension.

The young man caught her, mostly, as she came down. He got a good grip on her leg, and another on her wrist, and with one thing and another she didn't hit the concrete; rather, she thudded down onto a layer of wood chips underneath the bush.

"Holy cats!" he said, "Are you hurt?"

Emily lay stunned there for a second, tears leaking from the corners of her eyes, and finally shook her head.

"Wow. That was crazy," the young man said.

"I don't like heights," Emily said, hoping her nightmare would allow the ground to open and swallow her whole.

"You sure don't. But that's only sensible," he said, and sat down on the ground next to her. "Heights can kill you. I sometimes think that's their whole mission in life."

Emily's mission in life was to cease to exist. She could feel the warmth of this boy's hands on her wrist and ankle. His hands had been sure, dry, smooth. From somewhere came the unmistakable smell of cinnamon rolls. Bark chips bit into her back and thighs. She opened her eyes and sat up.

"Whoa, there. Don't get too excited," he said, looking dubiously at her.

"I'm okay," she said, "At least I think I am." His eyes were very dark. "I just lost my balance. Thanks for catching me."

"My pleasure. My hands were unoccupied at the moment."

Emily was thinking she might be able to get herself up off the ground now when the gnome stuck his head around the bush.

"What's this?" he said, in the same high nasal voice, "Two of my favorite people having a short siesta under a bush?"

"It's not… I mean," Emily started, but then didn't quite know what she meant.

"She fell," the boy said. "I caught her."

"Splendid," Goofer said. "I always knew you had quick hands, son, and an even quicker mind."

Son? This perfect specimen of young manhood was the gnome's son?

"Are you okay? Other than that you're growing wood chips from your back?" Goofer said.

Emily managed a weak smile. "Yes, I'm just fine. Thanks to your son, whose name I don't know."

"Nickel," he said, looking away. He pronounced it like "pickle." Nickel Guffrain.

"I'm Emily."

Goofer was already scrambling up the ladder. "Gotta get this banner hung," he said. "People are on the way."

"Rope's too short," Emily said, coming back to life. "I'll find some more."

"There's a pile of stuff like that inside; I'll show you," Nickel said.

A few moments later Goofer had the sign up and Emily and Nickel leveled it off with a few just-a-little-lowers and shorten-the-rope-three-fingerses.

Spoonerville Rotary Golf Tournament, it said, now that it was talking properly.

Emily thought now might be a good time to ask, "So, are you going to be working with your father today?" The prospect of spending the day in such company was quite a bit better than it had been just a few minutes before.

"No, I'm on cart duty. I get to shuttle things back and forth from the holes to the clubhouse, and vice versa. It's a pretty cush job, but the club likes me. Where are you assigned?" For the first time, he seemed to take in the fact that she was wearing a bathing suit. "Oh," he said. "You'll be with Dad, then."

"So he says," Emily said, "but I'm a little confused as to what this is all in honor of?"

"It's a golf tournament to raise money for the Rotary Club. We do one every year. You've never been to one before?"

Emily shook her head. His voice was melodic and smooth, already changed. "We make most of our money for the year on this. My dad is a committee chair, and he always has some crazy idea that makes huge money for the club. This year he's kind of outdone himself, I think."

Golfers had been trickling up from the parking lot a few at a time, but now the trickle had become a flood, and the registration table was frantically getting four-somes registered. A six-pack of volunteers, all in Rotary purple, handed the registrants gift bags stuffed with goodies. Carts flowed up from the parking garage below the clubhouse, and golfers climbed aboard, consulted their cards, and headed out onto the course.

Zoo came out of the clubhouse with a bullhorn. "Welcome, everyone," she said, and made a couple of announcements about the course of the day, and what the donations were to be used for (clean water for a village in Africa). She urged everyone to be generous with their money, but to be sure to have a good time.

"We'll start in ten minutes," she said, "When the clubhouse blows the horn. Shotgun start—everyone at the same time. Good luck and go win some prizes."

Goofer appeared behind the two teenagers. "Ready to go? Your mom is out on hole fourteen. She told me you were in my charge, and I was to treat you like my own daughter." He laughed uproariously at this.

Emily waited for him to finish. "You don't *have* a daughter, do you?"

"Nope! Only sons." He whistled at the nearest cart, which did not move. "Terrible training they give these things."

Hole Six. Also known as "the farthest point on the map from civilization." A shortish par four that features only one really interesting feature: a wide pond that takes the entire left side of the fairway and makes it a giant, golf-ball magnet of a torture chamber.

Also, it had ducks. And a couple of very large bass.

There was also Goofer's personal favorite feature: a block of lily pads floating about thirty yards out from shore. Why his favorite? Because it made a lovely, three-yard-wide target in the middle of the pond, ideal for chipping at.

But not golf balls—those cost money and sink to the bottom of the pond. No, Goofer had arrived at a different, possibly even more ridiculous fundraising idea. For five dollars, the intrepid golfers could take a potshot at the lily pads, and if they hit one, they got a free shot on a hole of their choice. For most of these guys, it was pretty close to a 50-50 chance at making the shot with a golf ball. But Goofer thought that was too easy.

So he made them do it with rubber ducks.

Rubber ducks do not fly true when hit with a pitching wedge. And since this added merriment to the proceedings, but also introduced a potential donation-killing element, Goofer added a wrinkle—for a dollar, they could try a second time.

With the same duck.

Which someone had to retrieve.

When Emily heard this part, she stood in the growing sunshine with mouth agape and now, finally, understood that the nightmare was all too terribly real.

"I have to do what?"

Goofer just smiled and went to welcome the first foursome.

"What were you going to do if no convenient victim showed up in a swimsuit?" she called to his retreating back.

He turned his head and winked. "The universe never lets me down like that."

Emily did have one thought, and that was that perhaps the golfers, who were mostly men of an age who would have daughters her age, would not want to subject her to having to dive into a muddy pond to retrieve a rubber duck just so they could try to earn a free shot.

Emily underestimated the lengths to which these men were willing to go to win the grand prize. To be fair, the top foursome did all get iPads and five tickets each to try to win the 72" flat screen. But still. Did they have no heart?

They did not. None of them. Emily got to the point where she didn't even bother getting out of the pond. She just found a convenient rock in the shallows and perched there, feeling like she should be singing "Part of Your World."

Torture. Pure sadistic torture. And Goofer's smile never wavered.

But she had to admit, all that silly verbiage he tossed out as easily as breathing had its effect on the golfers. They opened their wallets. Ducks flew. Emily retrieved them like an Irish setter. The Rotary Club brought in money like they had set up a printing press.

In one of the gaps, Emily said, "That's a lot of money for the club."

"We need every penny," Goofer said from his lawn chair under a spreading willow.

"But that money could do a lot of good in other places. These guys are all going to take this as deductions off their taxes. I've heard people argue that the government loses out on that money they could give to people in public schools or on welfare."

Goofer cocked his head to the side. "But you don't completely agree?"

Emily plucked grass and tossed it into the water. "No. I learned about this from a friend of mine. But it still seems to make sense. A lot of people argue the money needs to go to the government."

"Okay, let's walk through it. What do you think we as Rotarians are going to do with the money we take in?"

"Zoo said something about wells in Africa."

Goofer nodded. "That's right. Among other things."

"Still seems a waste. I don't think people should get a tax deduction for that."

Goofer laughed. He did that a lot. "Do you know why the government has that law in place?"

Emily did not. She chased an inquisitive bluegill away from her legs. They were going to get pruney soon. Maybe she should get out. But it was hot and the water was starting to feel pretty good.

Goofer saw that he wasn't going to get an answer. "The government takes in a lot of money. How much of it goes back out again? If I give the government a dollar, how much of that dollar actually goes to help people?"

Emily didn't know that, either, but she thought she should take a stab at it. "Ninety cents?"

"Try forty."

"Forty cents? Where does the rest of it go?"

"Down the bottomless maw of the state. Salaries, junkets, waste, fraud—the government can do it all."

"Charities do that, too," Emily said. She didn't want to agree with this man.

"Some, sure. But not all. And the best ones put all their money out there."

"And Rotary would be one of the best ones."

"It would. I wouldn't be here if it weren't." A cart approached, whirring through the rough. Goofer rose to meet it. But before it got there, he said, "The government gives Rotary and other service organizations tax-exempt status because the government once knew that private charities do a better job of using that money than the government does. A dollar of tax deduction is far better than a dollar sent to Washington, D.C." His smile broke out and he held his arms wide, as if personally welcoming the oncoming foursome to his private domain.

Emily tipped her head back and soaked up some sun. You know who else got tax-exempt status? Churches. Like the Our Lady church.

It wasn't her fault.

Nickel came rolling by after a couple of hours. He sat by the pond and chatted with Emily. He did have great eyes, and his freckles were dreamy.

But he was too much like his father. Too positive, too peppy. Eventually, they had nothing to talk about, and he went away. Emily just wanted to sit in the water and occasionally swim lazily out to retrieve an errant duck. She was getting paid for this, after all.

She *was* getting paid for this, after all... wasn't she?

The day wore on and Emily wore out. She got tired of Goofer's endless prattle and the earnestness of the golfers forking over their cash, as if it would do some faceless, nameless people on another continent any good at all. You know what would help? They could give the money to her. She deserved it. She needed it. Then she could make an anonymous donation to the church, and the window would get fixed. Taken care of. Done. Her life could go back to normal. The whole thing was stupid, anyway. This "working," the golf tournament, all of it.

She could just get into that cart over there and go. She didn't have to stay here. The last group was coming up to the tee. Let Goofer clean up the ducks. She'd make some excuse and maybe send a cart back for him. Nickel would come and get him, surely.

If you think she should leave early, turn to page 92.

If you think she should stick around and help, turn to page 30.

"How do we figure out which plan to choose?" Ethan said. "Emily's sounds pretty good to me."

"And Ethan's sounds like a winner to me," Emily said.

"That's one to one," Ethan said. "Maybe Uncle Ben should cast the deciding vote."

Uncle Ben laughed. "Not a chance. We have to do it together, so we have to decide together. But a decision like this calls for shakes."

Ethan looked up from his laptop. "That's my favorite kind of decision to make."

Three blocks away, the buildings of the office district gave way in one specific spot to a squat, one-story, crumbling brick building with a faded sign painted on the front that said, "Ziggy's." It stood like a gap in a row of teeth, hardly looking as if it was open.

But the rusty hinges on the front door creaked a welcome and the voice from the back called out, "Y'all come in." The old-fashioned lunch counter gleamed, and if the bar stools arrayed in front of it were worn and battered, they were clean. Uncle Ben drew up on the second chair from the left.

"Ziggy, I want the special," he called out.

"Ben? Have a seat and I got you," Ziggy called out of the back.

"You guys are old friends, I take it," Ethan said, sitting down to Uncle Ben's left.

Emily took the chair on the right. "It's a good idea to be friends with a guy who runs a diner."

Uncle Ben grabbed a straw from the dispenser and rapped it on the counter. "Not a diner. Take a sniff. Do you smell fries? No. All diners serve fries. Therefore, not a diner. This is that rarest of gems in the modern world: a true ice cream shop."

"Thas right," said a beefy, ruddy-faced man with dark hair pulled back in a cap, strolling in from the back, wiping his hands on a towel. He hung the towel on a small rack and turned to lean on a pair of hairy arms, a broad smile taking up so much of his face it was hard to see his eyes. "Ice cream. Y'all come to the best ice cream shop south of New York." He said it "Yawk." "Ben, you want the special? You sure?"

"I am. Don't I always?"

The counter rumbled as if an earthquake had begun. Emily realized Ziggy was laughing, so deep in his chest that she couldn't hear it. But she could feel it, all right.

"You do. Fugettaboutit, you always do." He reached behind him and plucked a deeply-scooped glass bowl like a river boat, from a sparkling stack. He drew an ice-cream scoop and twirled it, a gunslinger with his six-shooter, while flicking open a white freezer, curls of freezer smoke wafting upward into the humid July air.

"Out of curiosity," Emily said, "what is the special?"

The floor rumbled again.

"That means you have to wait and see," Uncle Ben said. "The special is actually what I wanted to bring you here for. It's a great lesson in marketing."

"How so?"

"Because the special is never ready for prime time," Ziggy said. "It's always changing, always sumpin' new. Sometimes it works, sometimes no. I never know until somebody comes in and orders it."

"Anyone in today for it?" Uncle Ben said. In response, a huge hand pointed up at a chalkboard on the rear wall, above the glasses. Chalked there were sixteen marks, ten on one side and six on the other.

"Sixteen. Pretty good."

"It's not bad, but I don't care until we get to twenty."

"Which you will."

"Which I def'nitly will."

"Are you going to keep it?"

"Time will tell, Ben. Time will tell."

In answer to the quizzical looks of the twins, Uncle Ben said, "Ziggy here doesn't decide if a specialty ice cream dish deserves to be a permanent until he tests it. If it makes the grade, then it goes in the permanent lineup. If not, then he tries something else."

"Why not just taste it himself?" Emily said.

"I do. I do. But my taste buds are froze from being here since I was six. What I like don' matter much. It's what the people like that matters. And how can I know what they gonna like, less I ask them?"

Written on the board above the tick marks were ice cream dishes like "Mudsucker" and "Six Kinds of Sour."

"Those made the cut, I take it," Ethan said.

"They did," Uncle Ben said. "He tested them. People liked them. They stayed."

"Lotta mistakes, though, behind the winners," Ziggy said. He lumped chocolate ice cream into the dish, then took a metal cup from behind him and tossed in a scoop of something green and another of a striped ice cream Ethan couldn't identify. He racked the metal cup in a blender and hit frappe.

"Here's the thing I like best about Ziggy. He doesn't wait to put something on the menu. He goes for it if he has an idea. He tests and he finds out what he can, then he keeps what works and gets rid of what doesn't. Most people wait, thinking through everything over and over, trying to make a perfect decision."

"Shouldn't you do that? You know, look before you leap, and all that?" Emily said.

"Ha," Ziggy said. "You can look if you want, but you still hafta leap. I like to look while I'm leapin'."

"My question is, until you leap, what are you looking at?" Uncle Ben said. "You don't get new information by analysis, you get it by trying things."

"That can be expensive," Ethan said. "What if your attempt is a disaster?"

Ziggy turned off the blender and poured the contents, which looked vaguely like vomit, over the chocolate ice cream.

Uncle Ben stared at it. "Like maybe this attempt," he said. "What's this one called, Ziggy? The Stomach Flu?"

Ziggy shook the floor again. "I won't name it until I'm keeping it. But I was thinking maybe 'Taste it Twice,' given the special nature of the dish, the color of it and all." He picked it up, plopped a cherry on top of it, and placed it gently on the counter in front of Uncle Ben. Fingers like sausages fished a spoon out of his apron and stabbed it into the concoction, where it stood like a fencepost, starting to sag, little by little.

"The attempt can be a disaster," Uncle Ben said, plucking the spoon from the dish and licking it off. His eyes narrowed. "But the disaster will cost a lot less if you just get it out of the way and move on. The big problem comes when you spend more and more money and more and more time trying to make something work that isn't going to. It might feel a little disappointing—maybe a lot disappointing—but it's far better than hanging on to something that ultimately isn't going to work. Better to make a change quickly and use the lesson of the failure to improve."

"So?" Ziggy said. "What do you think?"

Uncle Ben dug a huge, dripping spoonful from the squalid mess and shoved it into his mouth. He held up the spoon, eyes closed, while he savored it. Then he laid the spoon down and shook his head.

"Too much of the pistachio," he said. "It's a no for me."

Ziggy sighed a little like a hurricane blowing in, turned and chalked another mark on the right side, making it ten to seven. "I don' think I'm keepin' this one," he said. "But it was a good try. You kids want something?"

"I think I'll skip the special," Emily said, "But if you can make me a banana split I'll take it."

"Can do. What ice cream you want on it?"

Emily told him and he looked over at Ethan. "And you, young squire?"

"The Train Wreck for me."

Ziggy rumbled again. "You want to know what that is?"

"Nope. Probably better I don't ask."

"That's a bold man, right there. I will wreck your train but good."

A couple came into the shop, then a small family, followed by what looked like a baseball team, and all of a sudden the place was crowded. Uncle Ben and the teens moved to a small table in the corner and companionably ate their ice cream. Ethan's looked like someone had crumbled asphalt over whipped egg whites and then shaved an iron bar onto the pilings.

And it was delicious. No one else would try it, but Ethan wolfed his down with gusto.

"So there has to be a lesson in why you wanted us to come here," Emily said. "Or is it just that we don't know which of our ideas is likely to be a good one, so we should just do whatever."

"That's about it," Uncle Ben said. "Can you think of any information that would make your decision easier?"

"Sure. We could know how the whole thing comes out. Then it would be easy to decide."

"How about something that's possible to know."

The twins studied their ice cream. "I can't think of anything," Ethan finally said. "There's no real way to know which plan will work, or which we can even execute."

Uncle Ben nodded. "Then there's no reason to choose one thing over the other except for personal preference. You might as well flip a coin. But the point is that in this kind of situation, most people get paralyzed and don't make any kind of decision. They collect data and analyze, but the only thing that's going to tell you which one to do is to do them."

"Okay. Then I vote the next person that comes through that door makes the decision. If they order the special, then we do Emily's idea. If they order something else, we do mine," Ethan said.

"Works for me," Emily said. "Although I think that's a little slanted toward you. It doesn't matter, though. I think either one would work."

They kept their eyes on the door, and a minute or so later, a wizened old man came through, grey hair peeking out from under a faded baseball cap.

"He doesn't look like the adventurous type," Ethan said. "I think we're going to end up with a riot."

"Ziggy," the man said, "Your special today doesn't seem to be doing that well. I guess I better try it and find out if everyone in this city is just plain loco."

Emily twisted up a smile. "Looks like we're going to give those baseball people the silent treatment."

They did. Emily explained the whole idea to the assembled mothers Mrs. Douglass got together in her living room. They grumbled a bit and thought the whole thing was too weird to work, but Mrs. Douglass talked about the nonviolence of Dr. Martin Luther King and how this was merely an extension of that strategy. "They think we're going to blow up on them, get all crazy. This shows we're not like that. We have something to say, and we're going to say it without having to say anything at all."

But the idea didn't go down well with the neighborhood. In the end, only a few dozen people showed up. On camera it looked well enough, though the sparse crowd couldn't really fill up the screen as well as Emily hoped it would. She did think the dead silent crowd was effective, both on camera and in person. It was so quiet that they could hear the soft conversation of the baseball executives as they chatted over the proposed baseball stadium location. Watched carefully by the neighborhood, they pulled out maps and tried to have negotiations, but they were short and came to little. Even the washtub filled with ice and champagne, perched on the hill overlooking the river, didn't seem to be as celebratory as it probably was supposed to be.

As the delegation was leaving, one of the city administrators came over to Emily and put his hand over her camera. "Nice try, miss. You've accomplished nothing here today."

All of which was, of course, recorded by the secondary camera back and to her left. "We'll see," she said. "You're not going to knock down these people's houses without a fight."

But fights are won and fights are lost. The nature of a fight is that someone will lose, and in this case, all the viral videos and protest movements and community outrage were not enough.

The first problem was that the international baseball community chose Malantown as the site of the baseball tournament the following year. Once that decision was made, Malantown's decision was inevitable, and indeed, a few weeks later, the city council voted, 4-3, to move forward with the ballpark construction.

The twins, Uncle Ben, the Tuttle parents, and it seemed half the world packed into the council chambers to hear the "debate" on the proposition and to see the vote. It was an angry and a somber crowd that filed out of the chambers after the verdict was rendered.

"Well, we did all we could," Ethan said.

"Not good enough," Emily said. "We should have gone with your plan, Ethan. At least we would have gotten to scream at people. I think that would make me feel a lot better."

They sat in the fourth row as the seats emptied, slumped over and wiping back tears of frustration.

Finally, Uncle Ben blew out a breath and pushed up out of his chair. "I guess I better pack. We'll have to move in a couple weeks, it sounds like. That's going to be expensive."

Emily looked up in apprehension.

"No, no," Uncle Ben said. "You two have demonstrated your value. I'll be keeping you on as long as you want to work for me. We're in a lot better position than we would have been if you hadn't come along."

The twins' father hugged them. "I'm proud of you for doing what you did. Not your fault these things grind over the people; it's sort of how government works."

"Excuse me," a woman said, coming forward. *One of the councilmembers—Hawkins*, Emily thought. "Could I speak with you for a moment?"

"Councilwoman Hawkins," Uncle Ben said. "I'm sorry we couldn't persuade you to vote with us on this."

"There were, um, considerations you know nothing about that made it impossible. But I wanted to say two things to you. One, I admire what you did in support of your cause. You couldn't have worked harder or been more persistent in your messaging. It was terribly impressive to watch, and you got a lot of attention."

Emily looked disgusted and all Ethan could say was, "That's very nice to say when you've won."

"But the second thing is maybe more important, and it's something I don't think you know. Can I show you something?"

"Sure, we're not busy."

She sketched a smile and went to the dais, took up a sheaf of papers, and returned. Flipping through them, she stopped about halfway through at a highlighted section. She handed it to Uncle Ben.

"Read that," she said. "I think you'll like what you see."

"Pursuant to a demand from the International Committee of Baseball, the city of Malantown establishes a fund for relocation for any family displaced by the condemnation of the properties on which the new baseball fields shall be built. The fund may be accessed by any family on proof of former residence, and entitles any family to $10,000 in moving cost reimbursement and cash payment for defrayment of hardship." Uncle Ben sucked in a breath. "That's... This is incredible."

"We can't do anything about the displacements without giving up on the dream of having the international baseball tournament here. But we can make it so that the displacement hurts as little as possible."

"It's not what we were looking for, but it will help these folks," Uncle Ben said. "Unfortunately, it also hurts others. The government created the problem, now it's making all of us pay for it to help fix it."

Mrs. Hawkins took back the papers. "There are other ways to win than getting all you want. This probably isn't what you would have liked, but it's not nothing. And it would never have happened without you. The international delegation was impressed by your little demonstration when they came. I believe 'creeped out' was the term they used. They told me they saw the faces of your residents when they went to sleep at night. Their demand that we establish this fund was directly related to that."

"You didn't announce anything about this tonight," Uncle Ben said.

"We don't have the details worked out yet. But letters will be delivered by the end of next week to everyone in the district, and we'll make sure the money gets where it needs to go."

The twins bumped knuckles. "It's not nothing," Ethan said. It wasn't an ideal solution, but it was going to ease the problem for those affected.

"It's worth a lot to people we care about," Emily said. She looked at her parents, the beginnings of a smile breaking out on her face. "Can we go tell Mrs. Douglass before we go home?"

The End

"We should find others that got these notices. Maybe there's more information out there," Emily said.

Mrs. Douglass's attention sharpened. "You going farther down the road? Just the two of you?"

Emily shrugged. "That's where the people are."

"Not your people."

"Aren't people just, you know, people?"

"No, sugar. They are not. Your people are over there," she said, pointing back across the river, "and my people are over here. You may think you can mix them, but you can't. Not here."

"But, it's the 21st century," Ethan said.

The woman laughed, heartily and full. "They teach you that in school?"

"Well, yeah. There was a whole civil rights movement about it."

"And yet some folks are still putting their skin and our skin on a pallette and deciding which is the more valuable. I don't think I have to tell you which of us weighs more on that scale."

Ethan flushed. "Not me. I'm not one of those kinds of people. I'm trying to stop people who act that way. Isn't that why we're here in the first place? And how does it get fixed if we don't try to do something? Come on, Emily. We're leaving."

The twins blended together and headed back toward the open door. Shiana stepped up and tugged on her mother's apron. "But, Mam, don't worry about them. They have magic, like me."

"They'll need magic if they go left out my door. You can watch them, though. Maybe you can be their magic spirits and pull them out of trouble. They seem bent on getting into it up to their pale necks."

Shiana jetted out the door on the heels of the twins, who, sure enough, had turned left and had begun walking down the sidewalk deeper into the dead-end street. Across the street, the business district evaporated and in its place developed walk-up three-story apartments. Each stoop was crowded with people, young and old, all dark, and none friendly-faced. Their eyes followed the twins, suspicious and glittering.

Ethan swallowed. "Maybe Mrs. Douglass was right," he said.

"Oh, for heaven's sake. They're just people," Emily said. She broke off and marched up to one of the stoops to a woman seated on the bottom stair.

"Excuse me," Emily said, "We're asking people in the neighborhood about the eviction notices you got. Will you talk to us about it?"

The woman's eyes stayed long on Emily's face. "We didn't get one," she finally said.

"You didn't?" Emily felt Ethan come up behind her, and she felt less concerned.

"No. None of us did, did we?" she said, without looking up at the others behind her. But they all murmured the same, that they hadn't seen anything.

"Try down the road," she said. "I'm sure they got some there."

Maybe fifty yards farther along, teens without shirts shot a dirty basketball at two chain-netted basketball standards placed opposite one another across the street. Emily's steps slowed, but couldn't stop, not with Ethan's clopping along behind hers. A pair of the hoopsters glanced over their shoulders. One did a double-take and nudged his friend. They laughed and continued down the court. Rap blared from a box set on one of the stoops, attended by a pair of girls in faded jeans and cornrows.

When the twins drew even with the players, the game abruptly stopped. A huge young man, glistening sweat, stepped in front of them. He held the ball in a pair of meaty hands, dusty, as if covered in powdered sugar.

"What are you two doin' here?" he said. "Y'all don't belong here." He didn't sound annoyed, but it was clear he could easily get that way.

Emily tried. "We're trying to find out about the city evicting people from these, um, residences." She waved her clipboard at the apartments.

"DeShaun, you gotta 'residence' here?" said the behemoth.

A short, wiry kid, not much older than the Tuttles, snaked his way through the gathering group of players and said, "Residence? I got my home over there. What 'bout you, Carter? You got a 'residence'?" The group laughed. Edged sideways. Blocked the sidewalk.

"Nope. No 'residence.' Not any more. City said I have no place to live." He said it as if he thought it possible Emily was the cause of that.

"That's, um, that's what we want to ask about," she said, her voice small against the mass of faces ahead of her.

"What are you askin' about? You a baller?" DeShaun said, looking at Ethan.

"Used to be," Ethan said. "Now I play baseball more."

"Ho, baseball. That's right. City got to have their baseball. Right here, isn't it? You come to see how the field sits? Maybe put a base in the middle of my kitchen?" The neutral tone was gone, replaced by a growl.

"No, see, we don't want that. We want to stop it, if we can," Ethan said. It didn't register on their faces at all.

Carter spoke again, rumbling like a small earthquake. "I think you and yours already did enough here. You come down here with your clipboard and your faded jeans and you talk like you here to rescue us. We don't need you. Don't want you. No white kids are gonna come here and fix anything. It's been like this since forever, and you come here saying you're trying to help us? Naw."

Emily tried one more time. "We didn't come down here to start trouble. We just want to find out what the city told you about when you had to be out of your apartments. We think the city is wrong. Our uncle has a show, he might be able to do something to help."

"Oh, your uncle has a show." Carter's street accent evaporated. "Allow me to explain something to you, Miss. Your uncle's show has about as much chance to change the city's urban renewal policy as you have of dunking this ball over my friend DeShaun here. Do you think we haven't been to the meetings? Consulted our attorneys? Exhausted every legal channel? We have. The city's plan is cast in stone, and it will proceed over our dead bodies, if need be. Now. You have two options. You can turn around and take yourselves back to wherever it is you come from, or you can drop that clipboard and get on the court. But either way, we will have no further conversation about these apartment complexes, because if we do, my friends here are apt to become belligerent."

The group exploded in laughter. DeShaun slapped Carter on the back. "Man, why you gotta talk university to these poor children?"

"Just tryna be friendly," Carter said, a nasty edge to his smile.

A tiny voice, shrill and indignant, sliced through the noise. "Carter, you shut it. This here's my friend Emily. She has magic powers, just like me. Mam says you should respect folks. You want me to tell Mam you showin' disrespect?" Shiana pushed between the Tuttles, right up against Carter's huge frame, and tilted her head back to stare challengingly up at him.

"Miss Shiana, you need to get back home. Now." Carter kept the smile on his face, but it had lost all its charm.

"I'm going. You keep your ball to yourself. Come on, Emily. These guys don't like us very much." Shiana took Emily's hand and led her back the way they'd come.

Ethan kept close, mocking laughter echoing off the brick facades of the apartments.

"That didn't go well," Emily said, when they'd achieved a sufficient distance from the game, which had resumed. "I'm sorry, I don't know what I was thinking."

"Mama told you," Shiana said. "People don't want to listen to you. You don't look right."

Ethan kicked an aluminum can up the road. "I can't really blame them. You could hear it in their voices. They've been beaten up for so long they don't trust that the system can work for them."

"Funny thing is, I don't believe it either," Emily said.

"But you do," Ethan said. "Why else would we be here? We don't think the system works for us without pushing, but we still believe that if we can find the right lever, we can move things in the direction we want them to go. We believe we have power. We believe it because we're in power, or at least we look like, dress like the people who are. What if we didn't? What if the power was all in the hands of people that didn't look like us, so that even when we show up at a meeting, or a negotiation, it's obvious to everyone who is on what side of the argument? Would we believe we had power?"

Emily stopped walking and leaned against a lamp-post. "No. I suppose I wouldn't. I hate the idea of being unfairly advantaged."

"We can't not be what we are. We get a great education just because of who we are and what kind of family we were born into." Ethan sounded disgusted. He turned back toward the game and watched for a moment. "Maybe it's good to learn what it feels like to be powerless. Even if it's just for a second."

"So you have advantages. So do I. The question is, what do we do with those advantages?" Uncle Ben sat with his feet propped on his desk, a pile of chocolate-chip cookies mounded on a plate within easy reach. The twins slumped in chairs against the far wall, looking disgusted. But Ethan was eating, at least.

Around a mouthful of cookie, he said, "I don't know. Get rich or something."

"I'm not sure how my 'advantages' helped me much," Emily said. "I'm still stuck paying for a huge window, or did you forget that's how we got into this mess in the first place?"

Ethan took a swig of milk instead of answering.

"One advantage is that you're not in jail," Uncle Ben said. "If you'd been a group of black kids playing on that playground, what do you think would have happened? You might have seen as been vandals, not a couple of kids who happened to be playing baseball. Think about it. How far was that home run you hit?"

Emily shrugged. "I don't know. Far."

"Farther than you thought you could hit a ball?"

"Farther than I thought anyone could hit a ball," Ethan said.

"And what happens if the cops get there and look at that, and they also think it's farther than anyone could hit a ball. Then it's not an accident. Then it's vandalism, and you're in the back of a squad car, not riding home on your bikes." Uncle Ben stood up and handed Emily a cookie. "Carbs are good for stress. Eat."

Emily took one mechanically and began to chew, but only because she was ordered to. "I stayed and confessed. That made it believable. They wouldn't have arrested me."

"No, you still don't see. You stayed there and confessed because you expected to be believed. What if you hadn't expected that? What if your experience with the police is that they never believe a word you say? Then would you have stuck around? Heck, no. You'd have been out of there like a shot, because you'd know—or at least you'd believe—that no matter what you did it would end with you in juvenile detention. Latino kids are two or three times as likely to end up in juvie as white kids are. You expected they'd believe you, and they did. You speak the same kind of language the cops do. You were believable—this doesn't in any way lessen my admiration of you for owning up to it—and that comes from knowing you have advantages you can use. You got in no legal trouble. Your parents—both of them—were available to come down and stand with you. The priest believed you'd make good on your promise to pay back the window, even though he has no real way to make you do it. All this is built on a system of voluntary exchange that you take for granted, because you were born understanding it. You were born into it."

"But that's how the world works," Ethan said. "Voluntary exchange is what makes markets function." He pointed at the walls and out the door to the street. "None of this would be here at all without it. The apartments down the street wouldn't have been built without it. Everyone benefits from it, not just white people, or rich people."

Uncle Ben nodded. "That's not wrong, Ethan, but it's not complete. I can do business without trusting someone, but what do I have to have in place to feel good about the transaction?"

Ethan thought for a minute. "I don't know. Like, enforcement or something?"

"Exactly. Police. Lawyers. Contracts. All of those things are expensive. Did any of those things come into play in your window situation? No. The trust was there in place of them. Trust makes things cheaper. It increases the benefits to all parties involved. But where there is no trust? Transactions are slower. They take longer and they cost more, which makes the benefits smaller. Down the street, did you feel like there was trust there?"

"No way," Emily said, rousing herself a little. "They didn't trust me enough to even answer my questions."

"Even though you really were going to try to help them. So no transaction took place. No trust, no exchange. Our culture is built on the idea of trust, and people of the same tribe trust each other more than they trust people who don't look or sound like them."

"But that's true for everyone, isn't it? They trust each other more than they trust people who aren't like them?"

"Yes, but look at the starting position. You have money. Most of them don't. So if a transaction doesn't take place, you still have money, and they still don't. Caucasians still control most of the assets in this country. For instance, those buildings down there, the city bought them under eminent domain. Did any of the money go to the people that live in them?"

"I can tell by the way you asked the question the answer is no," Ethan said.

"That's right. They're all owned by some developer from St. Louis, or a real-estate investment company in Des Moines, or what have you. Not one of those buildings is owned by any of the people who live there. That's not atypical, but of course I don't have to tell you that it's very likely that none of the people who own them are black, either.

"For minorities to have access to property, they have to be able to enter into trusted transactions, and that's very hard, because most of the property is owned by those in the majority. It's taking a long time to get to where whites and blacks, Latinos and Asians trust each other enough to do business the way we think is 'normal.' It's not normal for everyone." Uncle Ben poured his glass full again.

"Which brings me back to my question—what do we do with our advantages? We can't get rid of them. So what is the honorable thing to do?"

Silence sat there for a long time, broken only by the faint ticking of the battery-powered clock. Finally Emily spoke. "We have to use them."

"Elaborate."

"Well, if we can't get rid of what we are, then we should use it. Not for ourselves, or not just for ourselves, but for everyone that doesn't have the same benefits. We should look for ways to bring those benefits to them. Do business with them. Listen to their grievances. Turn our benefits into their advantage, too. Because we all have some advantages, just by being Americans. They're out on the street playing ball instead of cowering in bomb shelters in Syria or something."

"Build on that."

Emily got up and began to pace as she talked. "The trouble is that so many people have done without some of the things we have for a long time. They probably don't trust that they'll ever be able to have them. They certainly don't trust us when we try to give ours to them—or at least share ours with them. We didn't get very far when we went down the street, but at least the one family was willing to listen."

"They didn't think we were going to get very far, though, did they?" Ethan said.

Emily shook her head. "And I guess they were right about that. But we can't just give up. We can do something to help those people. If we can find out how to stop the ballparks from being built, we can still help them to keep their homes."

Uncle Ben fired up his laptop with a click of the touchpad. "They won't thank us, even if we succeed."

"That's their problem. Doing something worth being thanked for is mine."

Armed with the information from the letter they had seen, the Tuttles attacked City Hall. They browbeat city employees, requested public information, pored over budget sheets. But they didn't have much to go on, and the City stonewalled at every turn. Information was redacted from disclosures. Phone calls were never returned. Meetings were endlessly rescheduled.

Uncle Ben produced a documentary about the whole project, disclosing all the information they had and interviewing families from the neighborhood. Shiana's magic powers were never more evident than in her short segment where she talked tearfully about not wanting to move again. The show got huge numbers of views and generated thousands of phone calls to the city administration.

The protests fell on deaf ears. Despite the delay in rolling out the "renovation," the day did finally come when the bulldozers rumbled down Compton Street toward the apartment complexes. Police in huge numbers set up roadblocks. Families, stuck between moving and staying, hoping the delay would go on forever, had scant days to pack before the demolition crews arrived.

Emily and Ethan walked the four blocks down the street to the Douglass's apartment and volunteered their services. Mrs. Douglass put them to work boxing up her books and cleaning the bathroom.

"Cleaning the bathroom?" Ethan said. "They're going to bulldoze the building. It's gonna be a lot dirtier after they get through with that."

"Doesn't matter," Mrs. Douglass said. "We're leaving it clean, not because of who they are, but because of who we are."

"Where will you go?" Emily said, laying another one of Shiana's drawings gently in a box.

"My mother lives in Cincinnati. We'll go stay there the rest of the summer and see where I can get work. Maybe down south somewhere. I've always wanted to see the Gulf Coast, and I love seafood. New Orleans? I don't really know. I can do most anything, and people always need accountants."

Emily got her father to come down with his van and take the family to the bus station. Despite the hard situation, the family was upbeat. Shiana chattered on and on about going to visit her grandma. Mrs. Douglass thanked the twins for their help and made sure Mr. Tuttle knew how big of a help they had been.

"Even though it didn't work, some of us are grateful that your kids cared enough to try to help save our homes." She turned to Emily. "Don't let the hard act fool you, darlin'. Everyone in those apartments watched your video. They knew who made it. And it mattered to them that you tried, even though they'd rather die than show you."

The Tuttles stayed until the bus came and took the Douglass family away, waving from the rear windows.

"It's not much," Emily said. "It's not even enough. But it's something. Even though it's going to take a long time, maybe if we keep trying to help, we'll get somewhere eventually."

The End

The Author

Connor Boyack is founder and president of Libertas Institute, a free market think tank in Utah. In that capacity he has changed dozens of laws in favor of personal freedom and free markets, and has launched a variety of educational projects, including The Tuttle Twins children's book series. Connor is the author of over a dozen books.

A California native and Brigham Young University graduate, Connor currently resides in Lehi, Utah, with his wife and two children.

The Illustrator

Elijah Stanfield is owner of Red House Motion Imaging, a media production company in Washington.

A longtime student of Austrian economics, history, and the classical liberal philosophy, Elijah has dedicated much of his time and energy to promoting the ideas of free markets and individual liberty. Some of his more notable works include producing eight videos in support of Ron Paul's 2012 presidential candidacy. He currently resides in Richland, Washington, with his wife April and their six children.

The Tuttle Twins and the Case of the Broken Window